CAMPAIGN 412

HÜRTGEN FOREST 1944 (1)

The US First Army's Route to the Rhine

MICHAEL. McNALLY   ILLUSTRATED BY DARREN TAN

OSPREY PUBLISHING
Bloomsbury Publishing Plc
Kemp House, Chawley Park, Cumnor Hill, Oxford OX2 9PH, UK
29 Earlsfort Terrace, Dublin 2, Ireland
1385 Broadway, 5th Floor, New York, NY 10018, USA
E-mail: info@ospreypublishing.com
www.ospreypublishing.com

OSPREY is a trademark of Osprey Publishing Ltd

First published in Great Britain in 2025

© Osprey Publishing Ltd, 2025

A catalog record for this book is available from the British Library.

ISBN: PB 9781472862297; eBook 9781472862310;
ePDF 9781472862303; XML 9781472862327

25 26 27 28 29   10 9 8 7 6 5 4 3 2 1

Maps by Bounford.com
3D BEVs by Paul Kime
Index by Mark Swift
Typeset by PDQ Digital Media Solutions, Bungay, UK
Printed by Repro India Ltd.

MIX
Paper
FSC® C047271

Osprey Publishing supports the Woodland Trust, the UK's leading woodland
conservation charity.

To find out more about our authors and books visit
www.ospreypublishing.com. Here you will find extracts, author
interviews, details of forthcoming events and the option to sign up for
our newsletter.

Images

All images, unless otherwise indicated, are from NARA.

Author's note

Firstly, and as always, I would like to thank my wife Petra, and children
Stephen, Elena, and Liam, for their support and understanding during the
whole writing process. Likewise my heartfelt gratitude for my successive
editors at Osprey – Nikolai Bogdanovic, Brianne Bellio, and Alex Boulton for
their support, guidance, and above all patience from proposal to delivery
of the manuscript. Again, my thanks to Darren Tan for producing three
pieces of artwork which truly invoke events during the first phase of
the fighting.

Closer to home, thanks to Volker Jung who one day fatefully suggested
that we travel to an open day at the 'Museum Hürtgenwald 1944 und im
Frieden' in Vossenack, to Albert Trostorf and the museum volunteers for
their support and kindness, and finally to those fellow members of the
Ormonde Military History Society who consented to my taking them
around the battlefield, and again, a second vote of thanks to Albert Trostorf
in making it a memorable visit.

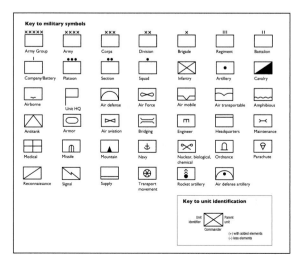

Front cover main illustration: The Battle of the Hürtgenwald, October
1944. (Darren Tan)
Title page image: A heavy machine gun and crew of the 9th Infantry
Division firing at enemy positions. (NARA)

CONTENTS

ORIGINS OF THE CAMPAIGN

In the summer of 1944, and in arguably one of the greatest gambles of World War II, the Allies launched Operation *Overlord*, a series of interconnected military operations intended to breach the seemingly impregnable walls of Hitler's *Festung Europa* and thereby secure a lodgment from where they could develop an additional theatre of operations, one which would not only ease the military situation on both the Eastern and Mediterranean fronts, but also place them within striking distance of Germany itself.

Preceded by a comprehensive program of active disinformation designed to divert German attention from the intended target area and by a series of limited military operations specifically targeting its aerial capability and transport infrastructure in order to prevent any immediate enemy counterattack, the main component of the plan – which took place on June 5–6 – involved the transport of some 132,000 seaborne and 24,000 airborne troops to secure a foothold on the Norman coast.

The risk was enormous as, quite simply, failure would not only see a crucial loss of both manpower and equipment comparable to the Dunkirk evacuation in 1940 but would also almost certainly preclude any possibility of a similar undertaking being made in 1945, by which time the strategic situation – both in Europe and elsewhere – could have changed considerably.

Having fought its way ashore against varying degrees of enemy opposition, the invasion force had achieved several of its initial objectives by June 12, but one – the city of Caen – would remain in German hands for several weeks, creating a bottleneck that thwarted several attempts to expand the British position on the eastern landing beaches. With the troops ashore, the Allied priority was now to secure a suitable facility for the movement of reinforcements and supplies, and, despite the creation of two prefabricated "Mulberry harbours," such transfers would continue to be made directly onto the beaches until the capture of the port of Cherbourg on June 26, but whose damaged facilities were to remain heavily restricted in capacity until mid-September. That said, the obvious problem with Cherbourg was that it was situated to the west of the landing beaches, and as the troops moved eastwards towards Germany, they would naturally be moving farther away from their supply hubs, the interim solution being columns of supply trucks whose lift capacity would be compromised by the need to carry their own fuel in addition to the planned cargo. As the campaign progressed, other ports suitable for the unloading of supplies would be captured but the one that truly mattered – Antwerp – was to stay firmly in German possession until early November.

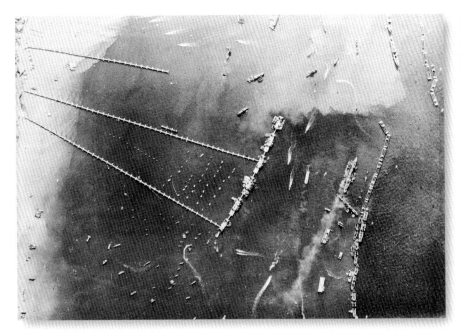

It was soon evident that not all of the invasion force's objectives would be achievable within the scope of the original timetable and thus it was decided to bypass enemy positions of strength which would then be left to wither on the vine until a later point in time when their capture would be a far easier proposition. As such, and as part of a planned realignment of Bradley's US First Army, VII Corps under Major-General Joseph L. Collins was instructed to cross the Cotentin Peninsula and by doing so cut Cherbourg off from any possibility of support or resupply. This movement was primarily considered as forming part of a general turning maneuver whereby Bradley's command would secure enough space to fully deploy and then ultimately wheel into the German left flank around Mortain.

At the other end of the Allied beachhead, British Second Army had begun its own preparations for a breakout to the southeast. The initial attack, Operation *Perch*, was intended as a pincer movement whereby the British I and XXX Corps would envelop Caen from both east and west, but was called off on June 13 when delays caused by heavy seas in the English Channel meant that the follow-up units were unable to deploy in accordance with the operational timetable. On the right flank, the 50th (Northumbrian) Division obtained a signal success when it mauled the German 352. Infanterie Division, thereby creating a significant gap in the enemy lines – but an attempt at exploitation by the 7th Armoured Division came to naught after the Battle of Villers-Bocage, and the British armor was withdrawn on June 14.

In the following days, the weather over the Channel worsened significantly, delaying the further transfer of supplies and reinforcements for almost a full week, forcing the Allies to concentrate much of their attention on consolidating their existing positions rather than pushing farther inland.

On June 26, 21st Army Group launched Operation *Epsom*, another attempt to flank Caen and render the German defense untenable by seizing high ground to the south of the city. Preceded by preliminary bombing by the RAF, the attack involved three British corps – I, VIII, and XXX – directly supported by over 700 guns, together with close air support and

Men of the US 60th Infantry Regiment advancing with support from a Sherman M4A1 Rhino. Note the Culin hedge cutter and the appliqué armor welded to the turret for extra protection.

shore bombardment by ships of the Royal Navy. Despite this overwhelming firepower, a dogged German defense was able to halt the British advance, but at the high cost of over 3,000 men and 120 tanks, the Allied high water mark being a temporary presence across the river Odon.

A week later, the British launched Operation *Charnwood*, a direct attack through Caen by I Corps, while VIII Corps moved simultaneously against the enemy positions to the west of the city. As before, the attack was preceded by a heavy aerial bombardment intended to pin the German forces – principally the 12. SS-Panzer Division "Hitlerjugend" and the 16. Luftwaffe Felddivision – in position and prevent them from disengaging and successfully withdrawing south of the Orne. The attack began on July 8 under cover of a creeping artillery barrage, and although the British troops had successfully reached the outskirts of Caen by late evening, they were unable to prevent the Germans from breaking contact as VIII Corps' attack had been halted by the presence of German heavy armor.

For the next week, the Allies sought to husband their strength, assimilating replacements and reinforcements, during which time planning began for a two-pronged offensive that would facilitate an Allied breakout from their current positions.

To the west, and having successfully isolated the German garrison of Cherbourg from any support, Omar Bradley's US First Army was to conduct Operation *Cobra* completing the conquest of the Cotentin Peninsula as far south as the port of Avranches, thereby creating the possibility of further Allied expansion both into Brittany and the Loire valley as well as posing a tangible threat to the now open left flank of the German 7. Armee. To the east, and supported by the newly arrived Canadian II Corps, the British Second Army under Sir Miles Dempsey was to maintain pressure on the enemy forces contesting the Allied occupation of Caen. Codenamed Operation *Goodwood*, Dempsey's original objective was to maneuver around the eastern suburbs in order to reach more open terrain to the south, which was more favorable to armored operations, before driving upon Falaise. During the final planning stages, Montgomery amended Dempsey's orders, so that *Goodwood* became a limited attack that he hoped would cause the enemy to commit precious reserves in order to block a possible armored thrust towards Paris. The rationale for this was that the more enemy troops committed against Dempsey, the less would remain to face Bradley, whose operation was arguably the more critical to the success of an Allied breakout. In addition, it was clear that of all the advantages held by the Allies, perhaps the most important of all was their ability to replace their losses at a far faster rate than the Germans, who not only had to deal with lower levels of production but also had to contend with the attentions of the dreaded *"Jabos"* – their nickname for the Allied ground-attack aircraft or *Jagdbomber* – whose mere presence ensured that the Germans moved their forces predominantly during the hours of darkness.

Under cover of a massive aerial and naval bombardment, *Goodwood* commenced on July 18, but progress was slow, delays being caused not only by a dogged German defense, but also by bottlenecks at the main bridging points across the Orne. After an advance of a mere 11km (7 miles), the operation was called off on July 20, having achieved little more than its secondary purpose of acting as a lightning rod for the German forces. It was soon bookended by two events which would now shape the next phase of the campaign in Normandy.

On July 17, the day before Dempsey launched his attack, an Allied combat air patrol operating near the inauspiciously named Sainte-Foy-de-Montgommery spotted and engaged a solitary German staff car, which was badly damaged in the strafing run and crashed, throwing its passenger – Generalfeldmarschall Erwin Rommel – from the vehicle. Suffering severe head injuries, the field marshall was taken first to a local military hospital for immediate surgery and

As members of a US patrol advance past a farm building, one of them studies the terrain ahead for enemy activity.

then transferred to a hospital in Germany, with his duties being temporarily assumed by his immediate superior, Günther von Kluge, OB West – the overall commander of all German forces in occupied Western Europe.

As if acting almost in accordance with Montgomery's wishes, Kluge quickly ordered the commitment of two of his precious armored formations – the "Hitlerjugend" and the 21. Panzer Division – in a forlorn attempt to blunt the Allied spearheads. It was a necessary expediency which, while yielding a decidedly Pyrrhic victory with both sides losing around 400 armored vehicles, nonetheless succeeded in its objective of obliging the Allies to break off their attack. But it was a series of reports coming from both Berlin and the Wolfsschanze in East Prussia that was to have greatest import: that on July 20, Hitler had been assassinated and a cadre of disaffected officers and opposition politicians had taken over the government.

After a few days, it became clear these reports had been gravely overexaggerated, with the Führer surviving the attempt on his life at the cost of a number of minor wounds. The most immediate result of the affair was a bloody purge of those

Breakout from Normandy, July–August 1944

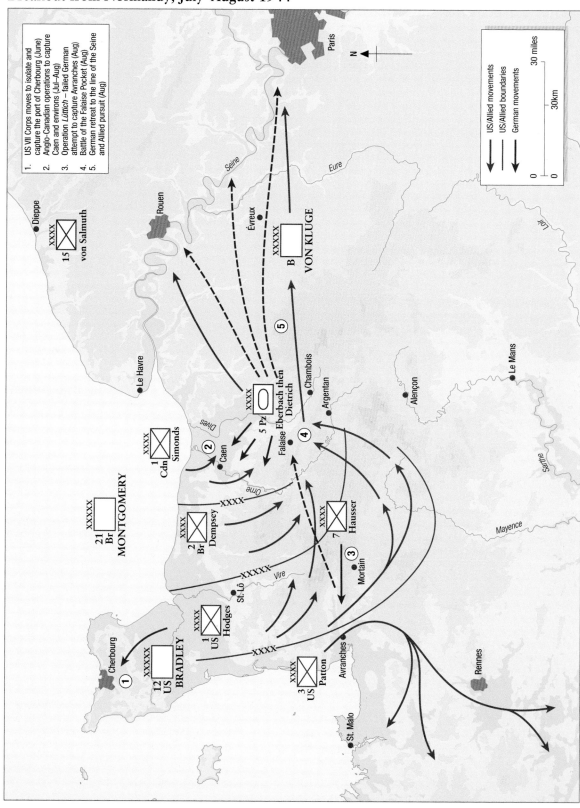

1. US VII Corps moves to isolate and capture the port of Cherbourg (June)
2. Anglo-Canadian operations to capture Caen and environs (Jul–Aug)
3. Operation *Lüttich* – failed German attempt to capture Avranches (Aug)
4. Battle of the Falaise Pocket (Aug)
5. German retreat to the line of the Seine and Allied pursuit (Aug)

US/Allied movements
US/Allied boundaries
German movements

30 miles

30km

N

Paris

Seine

Eure

Loir

Dieppe

XXXX
15
von Salmuth

Rouen

Le Havre

Évreux

XXXXX
B
VON KLUGE

5

Chambois

Argentan

Alençon

Le Mans

Sarthe

Mayence

XXXX
1 Cdn
Simonds

2

Caen

Dives

Falaise Eberbach then Dietrich

4

5 Pz

XXXXX
21 Br
MONTGOMERY

Orme

XXXX

XXXX
2 Br
Dempsey

XXXX
7 Hausser

XXXXX
Vire

3

Mortain

St. Lô

XXXX
1 US
Hodges

XXXXX
12 US
BRADLEY

Cherbourg

1

XXXX
3 US
Patton

Avranches

St. Malo

Rennes

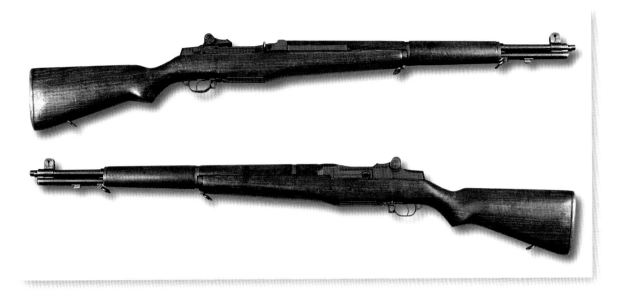

considered to be disaffected or opponents of the regime which would soon be underway.

Towards the end of the month, and with the enemy position greatly strengthened by Bradley's eventual success in securing the Cotentin Peninsula, the scene was set for a German counterstroke of almost Wagnerian conception; contrary to his own assessment of the military situation and his suggestion that German forces in Normandy withdraw to a new defensive position based on the line of the river Seine, Kluge was instructed to launch an armored attack – to be codenamed Operation *Lüttich* – towards Avranches and cut the enemy armies in two.

From his headquarters, Hitler now decreed that eight of the nine available panzer divisions, together with the local Luftwaffe reserve of over 1,000 aircraft, be committed to its execution. However, these instructions would be impossible to comply with given the necessity of simultaneously committing sufficient forces to contain the Anglo-Canadians. In the end, the attack was launched by a force of four armored divisions (2. and 116. Panzer Divisions together with elements of the 1. and 2. SS-Panzer Divisions "Leibstandarte" and "Das Reich") to be supported by two infantry divisions and a number of improvised Kampfgruppen drawn from the remnants of the Panzer "Lehr" Division.

The German attack began during the night of August 6/7, and although the Allies had already successfully intercepted and decoded a number of enemy radio transmissions, the attacking columns were still able to achieve a modicum of surprise, if only due to the fact that these intercepts had had to travel down the Allied chain of command, and thus by the time that they were received at the front lines, they were already redundant.

Daybreak, however, brought another side to the story, and as Allied fighters prevented the Luftwaffe from intervening in any constructive form, their ground attack aircraft enjoyed total air superiority over the battlefield and were soon wreaking havoc amongst the German ground forces with commentators from both sides referring to it being an object lesson in how airpower alone could defeat a major ground offensive. Despite this, the Germans still came agonizingly close to reaching their objective – their lead

US M1 Garand rifle (.30-06 cal), the standard weapon of the infantry companies. (Armémuseum [The Swedish Army Museum], CC BY-SA 4.0 https://creativecommons. org/licenses/by-sa/4.0, via Wikimedia Commons)

The debris of defeat – wreckage of a German PzKpfw IV.

elements stalling some 3km (2 miles) from the outskirts of Avranches – when the choice before them became one of survival or destruction.

Like *Wacht am Rhein*, a similarly ill-conceived offensive which would in fact take place some six months later, *Lüttich* would prove to be nothing more than an abject waste of resources that would have been far better deployed elsewhere and now, as the westward advance turned to an eastward withdrawal, it became a simple question of whether the retreating forces could affect a junction with the German front lines before being caught by the inevitable enemy pursuit. In an effort to prevent this, Hitler ordered that another attack be made, this time in the direction of Mortain. Once more, the German attack failed and the disorganized *Landser*, the ordinary foot soldiers, fell back towards what would become possibly the defining engagement of the Normandy Campaign: *die Kesselschlacht von Falaise* – the Battle of the Falaise Pocket.

With its armored reserves fully committed, and with a line of troops extending dangerously westwards into enemy-occupied territory, Heeresgruppe B stood in an untenable position that hovered on the brink of disaster, the only saving grace being that Allied fighters and ground attack aircraft were unable to operate during the hours of darkness, granting the Germans a reprieve from continual attack and offering a short window where they could move in relative safety. Perhaps the best appraisal of the situation came from Omar Bradley, who stated that, "This is an opportunity that comes to a commander not more than once in a century. We're about to destroy an entire hostile army and go all the way from here to the German border."

Bradley's comments were ambitious, displaying a sense of optimism that already pervaded the Allied High Command. They were now on the cusp of a pivotal moment, one that would signal an enemy collapse in Normandy and lead to their eventual defeat in the west. Accordingly, and in anticipation of a general German withdrawal, instructions were given for both Allied army groups to advance on a series of different axes, converging in the region of

Falaise–Chambois, thereby encircling and facilitating the capture of a significant number of enemy troops, the commencement of these operations having been naturally wrong-footed by the German offensive towards Avranches.

In an attempt to stabilize the front, and under continual enemy attack from ground and air, SS-Oberst-Gruppenführer Josef "Sepp" Dietrich and SS-Oberst-Gruppenführer Paul Hausser, in command of the German 5. Panzerarmee and 7. Armee respectively, ordered a concentration of troops around Falaise, the former facing off against the Anglo-Canadians moving south from Caen, with the latter tasked with holding off the Americans who had by now entered the Loire valley, far to the south of the German salient.

On August 15, and with the Allied advance gaining momentum, Kluge came dangerously close to sharing Rommel's fate when his staff car was attacked by Allied aircraft and, as a result, he lost contact with his headquarters for several crucial hours during which time Hitler convinced himself that, despite all of his recent protestations to the contrary, OB West was not as loyal as he claimed to be. When Kluge then demurred in following the Führer's next order to attack, he was immediately relieved of both commands and ordered to report to Berlin. Believing that he had been implicated in the ongoing investigation into the July Plot, and that his recall was but a prelude to a show trial and execution, Kluge chose to commit suicide, leaving a final note professing both his personal loyalty and expressing the view that the only real option for Germany at this stage of the war was a negotiated military settlement.

Having been likewise summoned to Berlin, but in his case to be rewarded for his recent successes on the Eastern Front, Kluge's successor was to be Generalfeldmarschall Walter Model, perhaps Germany's most capable defensive commander of the war, whose ability in seemingly being able to salvage the most impossible of situations had led to his gaining the sobriquet *"der Feuerwehrmann des Führers"* – "the Führer's Fireman."

Without waiting to receive a "sanitized" situation report from the staff in Berlin, Model opened direct communication with his new headquarters, and while the results of these conversations depicted a situation that was far from encouraging, the problems facing Germany were not – in his opinion – insurmountable, and on his own authority he gave orders for a further withdrawal to the Seine. Temporary command of the army group was now given to Hausser, arguably the most capable and experienced of Model's new subordinates. It would be his task to plan and implement the withdrawal until his commanding officer arrived from Berlin.

The immediate problem was that, with the abject failure of *Lüttich*, not only had the Germans suffered severe, potentially irreplaceable losses, but the Allies were able to capitalize on all their advantages. While the Anglo-Canadians may have been making slow progress in the adverse terrain around Caen, the Americans had successfully broken out into the open countryside of the Cotentin, thereby creating the very real possibility of a drive on Paris from the southwest, an eventuality which simply made a successful German defense in Normandy almost impossible.

By August 19, and under enemy attack from all points of the compass, the bulk of the German forces had been compressed into a triangular position between Falaise and Argentan, their sole hope of escape being a corridor across the river Dives near Chambois, which was soon closed by Allied forces. The only option for Model – who had by now assumed personal command of the battle – was to follow a practice developed on the Eastern Front, whereby the encircled troops were to attempt a breakout to the east while armored forces outside of the pocket would simultaneously attack westwards in order to catch the enemy between two fires and open an escape route.

The following morning, elements of the 2. and 9. SS-Panzer Divisions ("Das Reich" and "Hohenstaufen") launched an attack from outside of the pocket, while an armored thrust from within (10. and 12. SS-Panzer and 116. Panzer Divisions) fought its way to meet up, eventually breaking the Allied cordon and facilitating the escape of a significant body of friendly troops.

Heavy fighting continued throughout August 20 and 21, with the Germans launching attacks of increasing desperation as their numbers dwindled – at Mount Ormel, Polish troops would lose some 351 men and 11 tanks while the German losses, predominantly from the ranks of the "Hitlerjugend" numbered over 1,500. The only tangible effect of the engagement was that, having finally expended all of their ammunition, the exhausted Poles could act only as spectators as the enemy troops fled eastwards to safety.

To all intents and purposes, the Battle of the Falaise Pocket, and thus the Normandy campaign, was now over, with estimates differing greatly not only as to the damage suffered by the Wehrmacht forces but also the manner in which the damage was inflicted. Purely with regard to the pocket itself, a fair estimate would be to suggest that the German forces had lost a total of around 50,000–60,000 men, together with almost all of their armor and heavy equipment, and that a similar number were able to successfully reach friendly lines. There are two caveats to this, however. The first is that these estimates do not take into account any losses sustained during the fighting from June 6 to date and thus it must be assumed that the total loss of raw manpower and materiel was almost prohibitive, but it is the second of these qualifications that is arguably the more important, in that Heeresgruppe B was able to extricate a significant number of shattered command elements from the debacle, formations which could be quickly fleshed out with replacements and be sent back into the field in a relatively short period of time.

Having disengaged, both sides now needed to reorganize and resupply, and it was during this period of hiatus that the Allies received another boost. Despite having made the necessary preparations, General Dietrich von Choltitz, the German commandant of Paris, was unwilling to follow Hitler's *Trümmerfeldbefehl* of August 23, which would have seen not only mass deportations but also the wanton destruction of many key parts of the city. The original order stated that were Paris to fall into enemy hands, it should be only as a pile of smoking rubble. Instead, and following discreet backstairs diplomacy, Choltitz indicated that under certain conditions which would guarantee the lives of the troops under his command he would be willing to surrender the city to the Allies. Having received the requisite guarantees, he declared Paris to be an "open city," and on August 25 surrendered his command to Major-General Jacques-Philippe Leclerc of the Free French Forces.

Although the capture of Paris had not been one of Eisenhower's primary objectives, all of which had been predicated on the destruction of the German forces and their ability to prosecute the war, a single stroke of Choltitz's pen had irrevocably shifted the military situation in France in the Allies' favor, the possession of the French capital meaning that the Seine no longer constituted a viable obstacle. Only a further withdrawal would allow Model to once again stabilize the front.

A further consideration was that the position of Generaloberst Blaskowitz' Heeresgruppe G, currently engaged in containing the Allied advance from southern France, had also become more precarious and would likewise require a tactical realignment before it became engaged from multiple directions. In effect, there was no longer any possibility that the Germans could contain the Allied advance. Instead – and more or less until winter came – the tempo of the campaign would be dictated by a combination of their superior numbers and superior mobility. The only factor that could truly hinder the speed of the Allied advance was that, until a suitable port facility had been captured, all supplies would still need to be brought forward from the invasion beaches and Channel ports with the motor columns consuming almost as much materiel as they delivered to the forward areas.

The Red Ball Highway – the Allies' vital lifeline bringing much-needed supplies to the front line.

As August drew to a close, optimism in the Allied ranks was high, with the official history of the US First Army later recording:

By the beginning of September, the enemy had been driven back from the line of the Seine and that his hopes of holding the Somme-Marne line had been shattered. There had been a considerable deterioration of the enemy situation in the west. Captured documents showed that Field Marshall Model, who had succeeded von Kluge on 20 August, continued to issue futile orders to his disorganized forces. It was obvious that his orders were out of date before they could be issued to lower echelons. The enemy was told to occupy lines on the map when the Allied forces were already well beyond them. To say the least, confusion was supreme in the Headquarters of C-in-C west. Equally, the corps and divisions under C-in-C west were no longer a cohesive force, but a number of fugitive battlegroups disorganized and demoralized, and painfully short of equipment and arms. To back them up, Hitler continued to move into the rapidly diminishing area of Model's command, the scanty remains of reserves available in Germany. The enemy, in fact, had been out-generaled and out-fought and was no longer in a position to offer serious resistance to our forces on any line short of the West Wall. The rate of his withdrawal was dependent, not on how long he was ordered to defend a position, but rather on our own ability to keep moving despite the gasoline shortage.

The race for the Rhine, August–September 1944

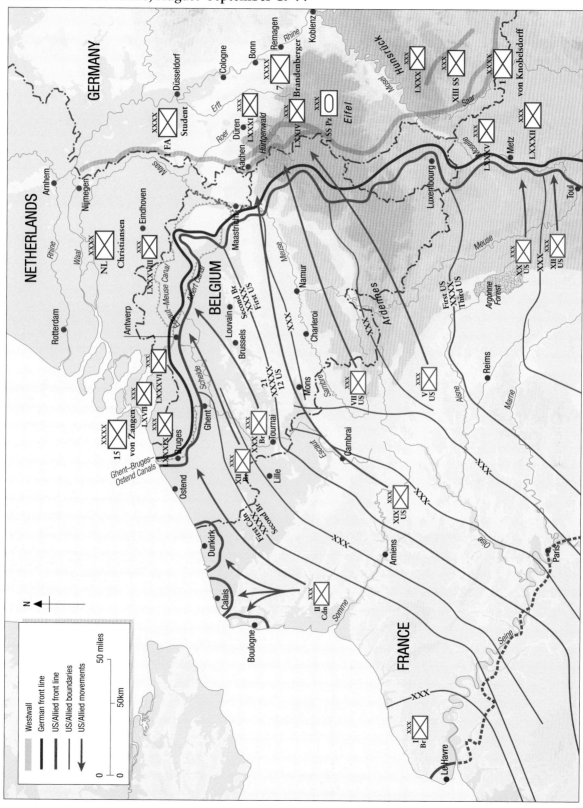

CHRONOLOGY

June 6   Operation *Overlord* – Allied invasion of Western Europe.

June 26   Operation *Epsom* – failed Allied attempt to break deadlock around Caen.

July 9   Operation *Charnwood* – limited Allied success nonetheless secures lodgment in Caen.

July 17   GFM Erwin Rommel (OB Heeresgruppe B) severely wounded in aerial attack. Rommel is succeeded by GFM Günther von Kluge who now holds both senior German commands in the west.

July 18   Operation *Goodwood* – failed Allied attempt to pass the river Orne south of Caen.

August 7   Operation *Lüttich* – failed German attack to cut off Allied troops in the Cotentin Peninsula.

August 12–21   Battle of the Falaise Pocket – Germans take significant losses but are able to break out towards Paris.

A heavy machine gun and crew (9th Infantry Division) firing at enemy positions.

Men of the 3rd Armored Division investigate the wreckage of a German StuG III Ausf.G assault gun. Produced en masse, these vehicles provided hitting power at a lower cost than conventional tanks.

August 19	Kluge commits suicide due to fears regarding the July Bomb Plot, he is succeeded in his offices by GFM Walter Model.
August 23	General Dietrich von Choltitz, commander of Paris, declares it an "open city" and begins negotiations for its surrender to the Allies.
September 2	US First Army crosses into Belgium
September 12	Lt Gen. Courtney Hodges orders a "reconnaissance in force" across First Army's front, the purpose being to test the German positions without bringing on a major engagement. Several American patrols cross into German territory, bringing back differing reports about German preparedness.
September 13	Beginning of American "reconnaissance in force."
	Advance elements of the 3rd Armored Division engage German forces at Roetgen and break through the enemy lines the following day.
September 14	Advance continues all across First Army's sector – beginning of the Battle of the Hürtgenwald, the fighting continuing through to February 1945.

OPPOSING COMMANDERS

AMERICAN

Unlike many of his contemporaries, **Lieutenant-General Courtney Hicks Hodges**' (1887–1966) military career had literally begun at the bottom when, in 1906 and having previously dropped out of the academy at West Point, he enlisted as a private soldier. Diligent, he was quickly promoted to sergeant before successfully passing the officers' entrance exams, joining the 13th Infantry as a second lieutenant.

Lieutenant Hodges first saw action during the Pancho Villa Expedition of 1916, before joining the American Expeditionary Force in France the following year when he distinguished himself in the St. Mihiel and Meuse–Argonne campaigns, where he was awarded the Distinguished Service Cross for heroism under fire.

Lieutenant-General Courtney H. Hodges, Commander US First Army.

At the end of the World War I, Hodges was appointed to the staff at West Point before serving in a number of staff and instructor positions, which culminated in his appointment as commandant of the Army Infantry School in 1940.

The following year, he received his promotion to major-general and was given command of X Corps, which eventually led to his subsequent promotion to lieutenant-general and the command of Third Army. As plans for an Allied invasion of Europe matured, Hodges moved to First Army as deputy to his friend Omar Bradley and after the breakout from Normandy in August 1944, with Bradley stepping up to command the newly formed 12th Army Group, Hodges succeeded to the army command.

Regarded by his contemporaries as a steady and dependable officer, Hodges' troops assisted in the liberation of Paris (August 25, 1944), and then with the failure of Operation *Market Garden* and Bradley's 12th Army Group now moving from its secondary role to the Allies' primary effort, he was then given the task of driving through the Hürtgen Forest to reach the Rhine near the city of Düren.

Major-General Joseph L. Collins, Commander US VII Corps.

In the bloody aftermath of the battle, elements of the First Army were able to exploit the German failure to fully destroy the railway bridge at Remagen and secure a bridgehead across the Rhine before the structure collapsed into the river. The laying of pontoon bridges allowed additional forces to transit the Rhine, and soon the Americans held a 40km-long (25-mile) section of its eastern bank. With the Rhine behind them, the First and Ninth Armies wheeled to defeat the remnants of Heeresgruppe B in the Ruhr Pocket, before conducting a symbolic linkup with Red Army forces near Torgau on the river Elbe.

On April 15, Hodges received his fourth star and First Army was redeployed to the Pacific for the proposed invasion of Japan, which was precluded by its surrender in August 1945. This would mean that Hodges was one of the few officers to witness the official surrender of each of the principal Axis powers. He retired from the army in March 1949 and passed away in 1966.

Despite having failed to obtain a congressional appointment to West Point upon his graduation from Louisiana State University, **Major-General Joseph Lawton Collins** (1896–1987) was still lucky enough to secure the position of "first reserve" should the original candidate fail to pass the entry exams. Fortuitously this is exactly what happened, and Collins entered the academy in June 1913, receiving a lieutenant's commission four years later.

After serving a short period as an infantry instructor at Fort Sill, he was promoted to captain in June 1918 and then to temporary major in September of the same year. Shortly before the end of hostilities he was given a battalion command, eventually being transferred to the Allied Army of Occupation.

Returning to America in 1921, Collins attended both the Infantry and Artillery Schools, before becoming an instructor in weapons and tactics at the former where he soon came to the attention of Lt. Col. George C. Marshall, the assistant commandant. After his tenure, Collins was promoted to major and appointed assistant chief of staff to the 23rd Brigade, then stationed in the Philippines.

Returning once more to the United States, Collins undertook a period of extensive study at the end of which he took up a teaching position at the Army War College (1938) leading to his promotion to full colonel and chief of staff to VII Corps in early 1941. The following year, aged 46, he stepped up a rank as a major-general, commanding the 25th Infantry Division during the Guadalcanal Campaign where he received the Silver Star for conspicuous gallantry in the face of the enemy, the citation noting: "... His example and words of praise and encouragement with which he continually encouraged his men in the forward units and spurred them on and contributed materially to the success of the offensive operation."

While Collins earned his laurels in the Pacific, discussion turned to the suitability of the current divisional commanders of the US First Army for their assignments in the proposed invasion of Europe, with none of the incumbents actually having any practical experience of amphibious warfare. In the end, it was decided that two of them would be replaced by officers with the requisite experience and so Collins – who was known to both Marshall and Bradley from their time at Fort Benning – was transferred to the European Theater of Operations (ETO) to fill one of the vacancies, that of the VII Corps where he had previously been chief of staff.

After the Normandy Landings, the VII Corps and its new commander – now known by a play on his initials as "Lightning Joe" – fully justified the faith in his abilities as they firstly secured the port of Cherbourg and then the whole of the Cotentin Peninsula before driving east to form the southern flank of the Allied attack on Falaise in mid-August. With the defeat of the Germans at this latter engagement and the subsequent capture of Paris on August 25, VII Corps forged its way towards Belgium and the German border, and a further battle of encirclement – this time at Mons – where it took some 25,000 enemy prisoners, further cementing Collins' reputation as both an intelligent and capable commander.

Following the heady drive across northern Europe, and with the Allied armies now standing within touching distance of Hitler's Reich, Collins – like his contemporaries – was to make an uncharacteristic error by simply underestimating the nature of the immediate task ahead, both in terms of terrain and also the enemy's ability to improvise new formations from the wreckage of others, but, unlike his peers, he would deal with the problems as they confronted him in an intelligent manner.

In April 1945, Collins, being regarded at the end of the war as being one of the best of the American corps commanders, was made a temporary lieutenant-general. Indeed, Bradley would later write that, "Had we have needed to create another ETO Army, despite his youth and lack of seniority, Collins would have almost certainly have been named its commander."

In later years, Colins would be involved in the establishment of NATO and served as army chief of staff during the Korean War. During World War II, his elder brother, James Lawton Collins, served as a brigadier-general in the Puerto Rico Department, while a nephew – James Lawton Collins, Jr – led an artillery battalion within his uncle's corps. A second nephew, Michael Collins, would serve as command module pilot for the Apollo 11 space mission.

A graduate of the Virginia Military Institute, **Major-General Leonard Townsend Gerow** (1888–1972) had the distinction of having been a recipient of the faculty's "Honor Appointment," an award which granted the individual an automatic commission as a second lieutenant in the Regular Army without further examination or qualification and, as a result, joined the US Army infantry on September 29, 1911, rising to first lieutenant in 1916 and then captain on May 15, 1917, shortly after the entry of the United States into World War I.

Major-General Leonard T. Gerow, Commander US V Corps.

A born administrator, Gerow's role covered the procurement of radio equipment for the American Expeditionary Force. Seeing action at the Second Battle of the Marne, St. Mihiel, and the Meuse–Argonne Offensive, he ended the war with a local rank of lieutenant-colonel, the recipient of both the Distinguished Service Medal and France's Légion d'Honneur.

After the end of hostilities, Gerow attended the advanced course at the Infantry School at Fort Benning, finishing top of the class of 1925 – one place higher than his friend, Omar Bradley. He then attended the Command and General Staff School at Fort Leavenworth where his study partner was a Major Dwight D. Eisenhower.

These two men's paths would fatefully cross several times, the next occasion being in February 1942 when Gerow – in the wake of the attack on Pearl Harbor and at that time Chief of War Plans Division on the General Staff – was promoted to major-general pending an appointment to a field command, with Eisenhower being selected as his replacement.

The outgoing officer reputedly greeted his former classmate by saying, "Well, I got Pearl Harbor on the book; lost the PI [Philippine Islands], Sumatra and all the NEI [Netherlands East Indies] north of the Barrier. Let's see what you can do."

It was a flippant aside that would, in time, come back to haunt him.

Despite the misgivings of George C. Marshall – now Army Chief of Staff – about Gerow's suitability for higher command, he nonetheless received command of the 29th Infantry Division and then, on July 17, 1943, that of its parent formation, V Corps.

A planner rather than a combat officer, Gerow was naturally heavily involved in the preparation of Operation *Overlord*, and when Eisenhower and Bradley elected to replace two of First Army's three corps commanders, it was his previous connections to both men that would not only keep him in his current post but maintain his profile throughout the latter stages of the war.

Gerow's image during the Normandy campaign had been a press officer's dream – he was the first corps commander to land on the beaches, and the first American officer of his rank to enter Paris after its liberation. However, his troops had been fought hard and had taken what many viewed as being excessive casualties, although others saw such losses as being inevitable, given the character of an opposed amphibious landing coupled with the nature of the terrain that had been fought over following the breakout from the beaches.

Again, Gerow was deeply involved in the planning for the big push to the German border and beyond, but on September 17 the past caught up with him when he was summoned to testify before the Army Pearl Harbor Board which was tasked with investigating the failures that had led to America's unpreparedness for the Japanese attack in 1941. Upon its conclusion, Gerow was censured for failing to keep the local commander – Lt. Gen. Walter Short – fully apprised of developments in the period leading up to the attack.

Although the man was chastened by this experience, his star continued to shine brightly, with Eisenhower not only placing him at number eight on a list of 32 general officers based upon the value of their conduct and service record during the war, but he also included him on a second list, this time of officers whom Eisenhower considered suitable for a transfer from the ETO to assume an army-level command in the Pacific.

Gerow ended the war with command of the newly formed 15th Army on January 15, 1945, and a retroactive promotion to lieutenant-general, backdated to the beginning of the year.

GERMAN

General der Panzertruppen Erich Brandenberger (1892–1955) joined the Royal Bavarian Army in 1911 as a junior artillery officer, rising to the rank of Leutnant – or second lieutenant – by the outbreak of World War I and, with the exception of a short staff secondment, he would spend his entire service on the Western Front, during the course of which he was wounded several times and was awarded both classes of the Iron Cross. At the end of 1917, Brandenberger was promoted to Oberleutnant and, early the following year, was given a battery command, serving in this role until demobilization at the end of the war. Like many of his peers, Brandenberger served in the Freikorps during the early years of the Weimar Republic, before receiving a commission in the Reichswehr as an ordnance officer, eventually being promoted to Hauptmann and given command of a battery in the 7th (Bavarian) Artillery Regiment.

In the summer of 1939, Brandenberger's unit was transferred to the Saarland on Germany's western border during the period known as the Sitzkrieg or "Phoney War" before it was incorporated into the newly established XXIII Armeekorps. This inactivity was not to last, and the formation was taken out of the line in preparation for the invasion of France in May 1940 (*Fall Rot*) where it took part in operations both in Champagne and on the Channel Coast. For his role in the fighting, he was promoted to Generalmajor.

On February 15, 1941, Brandenberger was transferred to the OKH Führerreserve, an administrative formation for officers pending appointment to senior command, and shortly afterward he was given command of the 8. Panzer Division in the run-up to the invasion of Russia. Attached to Heeresgruppe Nord, the division spearheaded the attack into the Baltic States, ultimately taking part in the fighting around Leningrad and Smolensk, its commander receiving the Knight's Cross of the Iron Cross and promotion to Generalleutnant on August 1, 1942.

In January 1943, and possibly due to the severe losses incurred by the Wehrmacht at Stalingrad, Brandenberger found himself once more moved to the Führerreserve from where he was initially appointed to the command firstly of LIX and then that of XXIX Armeekorps, which was serving in southern Ukraine as part of the newly reconstituted German 6. Armee. In the wake of the Battle of Kursk, Brandenberger led his troops with skill against the Soviet counter-offensive and, as a result, when the annual list of promotions was announced on August 1, 1943, he was elevated to

Effectively a wooden box filled with explosives, this German Schützenmine 42 would prove exceptionally difficult to detect.

the rank of General der Artillerie,[1] although this would later be amended to General der Panzertruppen, and for his conduct in the summer's fighting he was awarded the Oakleaves to his Knight's Cross.

Early in 1944, Brandenberger was further commended and mentioned in dispatches, the report stating that, "During the heavy fighting in the Nikopol area, German forces under the command of Generals Schörner, Brandenberger, Mieth and Kreysing prevented successive enemy breakthrough attempts during the extended period from 5 November 1943 through to 15 February 1944 causing significant losses upon the enemy with the fighting often taking place at point-blank range."

His service on the Eastern Front was drawing to a close, however, as at the beginning of July 1944 he found himself once again in the Führerreserve and on September 3, was given the command of the German 7. Armee, in succession to Heinrich Eberbach, who had recently been captured by British troops near Amiens.

Brandenberger would command the 7. Armee throughout the latter stages of the campaign in northern France and Belgium, the Siegfried Line Campaign, and the Ardennes Offensive, before being slowly pushed back towards and then across the Rhine, retaining his command until March 26, 1945, when – following a final transfer to the Führerreserve – he was appointed to command the 19. Armee on the Upper Rhine, ultimately surrendering his command to Lt. Gen. Edward Hale of the US V Corps at Innsbruck on May 5, three days before the official "Instrument of Surrender" was signed in Berlin.

Generalleutnant Friedrich-August Schack, Commander German LXXXI Armeekorps.

Like many young men of his generation, **Generalleutnant Friedrich-August Schack** (1892–1968) volunteered for military service at the outbreak of World War I, working his way up through the ranks as a platoon commander and then as both a battalion and regimental adjutant, having received both classes of the Iron Cross as well as the Bulgarian Military Order of Merit (5th Class).

Upon the cessation of hostilities in 1918, Schack was commissioned as a Leutnant in the Reichsheer, being lucky enough to remain in service upon its redesignation as the Reichswehr. Promoted to Oberleutnant on April 1, 1923, he was made Hauptmann five years later, at which time he received a company command. Further promotion to first Major and then Oberstleutnant followed, during which time he became a lecturer in infantry tactics at the Dresden Infantry School.

In late 1938, Schack was given command of a machine-gun battalion with which he led through the invasion of Poland and, during the winter of 1939–40, he was given command of the 392. Infanterie-Regiment, which he led throughout the campaign in the west and then into Russia during Operation *Barbarossa*, where he was awarded the Knight's Cross for his conduct during the capture of Salla in Finnish Lapland.

---

1   Army or Luftwaffe officers of general's rank were differentiated by branch of service, thus Infanterie, Artillerie, Panzertruppe, Fallschirmtruppe, etc.

A Sherman M4A2 tank, equipped with a bow-mounted E4-5 flamethrower, engages enemy positions. *Panzersperren* can be seen to the left of the image.

The following year, he was transferred to the command of the officers' training school at Döberitz before receiving his promotion to Generalmajor and command of the 216. Infanterie Division on July 1, 1943, shortly before the commencement of Operation *Zitadelle*. Decimated in the fighting around the Kursk Salient, Schack's battered division was transferred to France to refit, ultimately becoming the replacement cadre for the newly reconstituted 272. Infanterie Division of which Schack was given command, being promoted to Generalleutnant on New Year's Day 1944.

During the Allied invasion of Normandy, Schack's command fought itself to virtual destruction during the bitter fighting around Caen before being withdrawn to Germany following the failure of Operation *Lüttich* and the collapse of the Falaise Pocket.

On September 4, Schack was given command of LXXXI Armeekorps, which was then occupying a defensive position southwest of Aachen, holding this position for some weeks before his eventual replacement by General Friedrich Köchling, who was in the process of being transferred from the Eastern Front. On September 20, 1944, Schack officially relinquished his command, the following day receiving the Oakleaves to his Knight's Cross before moving to the Führerreserve where he acted as a "caretaker" commander for several corps-sized formations during their reconstitution and reorganization. Finally, and in the closing stages of the war, he was given the command of XXXII Armeekorps on the Eastern Front.

By the outbreak of World War I, **Generalleutnant Erich Straube** (1887–1971) was already well established on the *Laufbahn*, or career path, of a Prussian officer. From a retroactive promotion to Leutnant in December 1914, he received steady promotion, ending his wartime service as a staff captain, having been awarded – amongst other decorations – both classes of the Iron Cross.

Fortunate to maintain his commission in the postbellum army, Straube assumed a company command before transferring to the Army Ministry in Berlin and from there to the Schwerin Military District. Here he remained

A US M1A1 Thompson submachine gun. (Wikimedia Commons)

for two years before taking up an appointment as a tactical instructor at the Infantry School in Dresden, during which time he received his promotion to Major.

In July 1933, Straube joined the Inspectorate of Military Schools in Berlin as chief of staff. Further promotions via his service at army headquarters ensued and, on June 1, 1939, he was promoted to Generalmajor, being appointed to the command of the newly formed 268. Infanterie Division, at that time stationed near the French border.

With much of the focus being directed at the German penetration of northern France and the Low Countries, on June 17, 1940, Straube nonetheless led his division against a section of the Maginot Line, breaching the enemy defenses and effecting a deep penetration into the enemy rear, for which he was awarded the Knight's Cross. This attack marked the high water mark of his service in France and his command was eventually redeployed to the east in preparation for the coming offensive against Soviet Russia.

Straube remained in command of his division for the first six months of the invasion, receiving a promotion to Generalleutnant before being transferred to the Führerreserve in January 1942. By the summer of that year, he was promoted to full general and given command of Army Group South's XIII Armeekorps.

Gravely wounded in early 1943, Straube was obliged to relinquish his command, and in late August was appointed to command the LXXIV Armeekorps in France. For his conduct in the German defense against the Allied invasion, he would later be awarded the Oakleaves to his Knight's Cross.

In December 1944, Straube assumed command of the LXXXVI Armeekorps, and the following month, having been unable to hold back the enemy attacks on the Maas–Rur defensive line, found himself brought before a summary court martial charged with treason and dereliction of duty, but the trial was abandoned before he could be sentenced, almost certainly escaping the firing squad. On April 28, 1945, in succession to Generaloberst Kurt Student, he was appointed commander of the 1. Fallschirm-Armee.

OPPOSING FORCES

AMERICAN

The principal Allied force engaged in the fighting for the Hürtgenwald was the US First Army, comprising three corps, namely V (Gerow), VII (Collins), and XIX (Corlett), each of which nominally contained two infantry and one armored division. That said, at the beginning of the battle, only VII had its full complement of troops, with V being in the process of receiving the 5th Armored from Third Army, while XIX had transferred the 79th Infantry Division back to Third Army from where it had been on attachment. Thus, when his forces entered combat with the enemy, Hodges had – on paper at least – a total of five infantry and three armored divisions at his disposal, a force of roughly 120,000 men. Of these, possibly 20,000 or so would have been deployed with Corlett's XIX Corps north of Aachen and would thus have left him with perhaps 100,000 or so effectives, split more or less equally between his two remaining corps.

As per its formal organization, each infantry division was composed of three infantry regiments – each of three battalions consisting of a headquarters company, three lettered rifle companies and a weapons company, while the armored formations contained one or more armored regiments, which were generally divided into all arms "combat commands," the active ones being listed as "A–C" with a possible fourth such formation listed as "R" for reserve.

Having fought their way across Europe to the borders of the Reich, it could be said that these were all experienced units, especially VII Corps' infantry divisions, both of which had been in the field since the Allied invasion of North Africa in 1942, but since the breakout from Normandy in July, the campaign had been one of relentless pursuit, the principal enemy being the ever-increasing logistical difficulties faced by the constantly moving columns, and the troops would soon encounter a combat environment that would tax the men to their utmost limits and – in many cases – beyond.

Like all of the higher Allied combat formations, First Army would enter the coming battle lacking most of the impedimenta that a modern, industrialized army requires in order to function to the best of its ability, but as the men fought their way forward, they would nonetheless demonstrate a facility for improvisation that would enable them to gradually surmount the obstacles – both military and physical – that would face them in the coming months.

GERMAN

During their retreat to the German border, the troops of Heeresgruppe B had been engaged in what can best be termed as a running battle of annihilation, prey to a faster-moving, better-equipped enemy with superiority in almost all areas of consideration. As a result of the failure of Operation *Lüttich* and the encirclements at Falaise and Mons, an almost prohibitive level of men and equipment had already been lost with nominal battalions crossing into Germany that were in reality no more than companies, regiments the size of battalions, or divisions that were no larger than a full-strength regiment. In order to bring some coherence and cohesion to the order of battle, many units were stripped down and their component elements used to sustain front-line combat units, their "redundant" command units were taken out of the line and used to form central cadres around which new units could be built, a practice that reputedly led to "9th Panzer" becoming army slang for an aggregate formation with little or no armor support. As such, Model was able to plug many gaps and stabilize the front line before the Westwall defenses could be breached.

Nominally at least, Brandenberger's 7. Armee contained three army corps – running north to south – LXXXI (Schack), LXXIV (Straube), and I SS-Panzer (Keppler), the necessity of the situation was that many units were simply thrust into the line outside of their parent formation's area of operations as the situation dictated. For example, the remnants of the 353. Infanterie Division were deployed within the city of Aachen, thus coming under the aegis of the LXXXI Armeekorps while in actuality it was in the process of being attached to the LXXXVIII Armeekorps. For Model, as army group commander, these considerations could be deferred until later, the overriding priority simply being to present a coherent defense. Nonetheless, as increasing numbers of German troops were captured by American forces, the results of Model's pragmatism would result in several formations being mistakenly reported in US after-action reports. For example, the German 36. Infanterie Division would be broken up in late August 1944 then re-formed as the 36. Grenadier Division, which itself would be broken up through losses and reinforced/reconstituted as the 36. Volksgrenadier Division in October 1944.

A German MP40 (1943 variant) with folding stock. Commonly, but erroneously, known as the "Schmeisser," it is perhaps the most easily recognizable infantry weapon employed by the Wehrmacht. (Quickload at English Wikipedia, CC BY-SA 3.0 https://creativecommons.org/licenses/by-sa/3.0, via Wikimedia Commons)

ORDERS OF BATTLE

AMERICAN

US FIRST ARMY – Lt. Gen. Courtney H. Hodges

V CORPS – Maj. Gen. Leonard T. Gerow

102nd Cavalry Group – Col. Cyrus A. Dolph III
38th Cavalry Reconnaissance Squadron (mech)
102nd Cavalry Reconnaissance Squadron (mech)
4th US Infantry Division – Maj. Gen. Raymond O. Barton
4th Cavalry Reconnaissance Troop (mech)
4th Engineer Combat Battalion
8th Infantry Regiment – Col. James S. Rodwell
12th Infantry Regiment – Col. James S. Luckett
22nd Infantry Regiment – Col. Charles T. Lanham
Divisional Artillery – Brig. Gen. Harold W. Blakeley
20th Field Artillery Battalion (155mm)
29th Field Artillery Battalion (105mm)
42nd Field Artillery Battalion (105mm)
84th Field Artillery Battalion (105mm)
28th US Infantry Division – Brig. Gen. Norman D. Cota
28th Cavalry Reconnaissance Troop (mech)
103rd Engineer Combat Battalion
109th Infantry Regiment – Col. William L. Blanton
110th Infantry Regiment – Col. Theodore A. Seely
112th Infantry Regiment – Lt. Col. Carl L. Peterson
Divisional Artillery – Brig. Gen. Basil H. Perry
107th Field Artillery Battalion (105mm)
108th Field Artillery Battalion (155mm)
109th Field Artillery Battalion (105mm)
229th Field Artillery Battalion (105mm)
5th Armored Division – Maj. Gen. Lunsford E. Oliver
Combat Command A – Brig. Gen. Eugene A. Regnier
Combat Command B – Col. John T. Cole
Combat Command R – Col. Glen H. Anderson
22nd Armored Engineer Battalion
85th Armored Reconnaissance Battalion
46th Armored Infantry Regiment
10th Tank Battalion
34th Tank Battalion
81st Tank Battalion
Divisional Artillery – Col. Douglas J. Page
47th Armored Field Artillery Battalion (105mm)
71st Armored Field Artillery Battalion (105mm)
95th Armored Field Artillery Battalion (105mm)

VII CORPS – Maj. Gen. Joseph L. Collins

4th Cavalry Group – Col. Joseph M. Tully
4th Cavalry Reconnaissance Squadron (mech)
24th Cavalry Reconnaissance Squadron (mech)
1st US Infantry Division – Maj. Gen. Clarence R. Huebner
1st Cavalry Reconnaissance Troop (mech)
1st Engineer Combat Battalion
16th Infantry Regiment – Col. Frederick R. Gibb
18th Infantry Regiment – Col. George Smith, Jr
26th Infantry Regiment – Col. John F. R. Seitz
Divisional Artillery – Brig. Gen. Clift Andrus
5th Field Artillery Battalion (155mm)
7th Field Artillery Battalion (105mm)
32nd Field Artillery Battalion (105mm)
33rd Field Artillery Battalion (105mm)
9th US Infantry Division – Maj. Gen. Louis A. Craig
9th Cavalry Reconnaissance Troop (mech)
15th Engineer Combat Battalion
39th Infantry Regiment – Lt. Col. Van H. Bond

47th Infantry Regiment – Col. George H. Smythe
60th Infantry Regiment – Col. Jesse L. Gibney
Divisional Artillery – Brig. Gen. Reese M. Howell
26th Field Artillery Battalion (105mm)
34th Field Artillery Battalion (155mm)
60th Field Artillery Battalion (105mm)
84th Field Artillery Battalion (105mm)
3rd Armored Division – Maj. Gen. Maurice Rose
Combat Command A – Brig. Gen. Doyle O. Hickey
Combat Command B – Brig. Gen. Truman E. Boudinot
Combat Command R – Col. Carl J. Rohsenberger
23rd Armored Engineer Battalion
83rd Armored Reconnaissance Battalion
36th Armored Infantry Regiment
32nd Armored Regiment
33rd Armored Regiment
Divisional Artillery – Col. Frederic G. Brown
54th Armored Field Artillery Battalion (105mm)
67th Armored Field Artillery Battalion (105mm)
391st Armored Field Artillery Battalion (105mm)

XIX CORPS – Maj. Gen. Charles H. Corlett

Deployed north of Aachen and did not participate in this phase of operations.

GERMAN (September 18, 1944)

7. ARMEE – General der Panzertruppen Erich Brandenberger

LXXIV ARMEEKORPS – General der Infanterie Erich Straube

347. Infanterie Division – Generalleutnant Wolf Trierenburg
Divisions-Füsilier-Bataillon 347
Grenadier-Regiment 860
Grenadier-Regiment 861
Grenadier-Regiment 880
Artillerie-Regiment 347
Panzerjäger-Abteilung 347
Pionier-Bataillon 347
526. Infanterie Division – Generalleutnant Kurt Schmidt
Grenadier-Ersatz-und-Ausbildungs-Regiment 211
Grenadier-Ersatz-und-Ausbildungs-Regiment 253
Grenadier-Ersatz-und-Ausbildungs-Regiment 536
Artillerie-Ersatz-und-Ausbildungs-Regiment 16
Pionier-Ersatz-und-Ausbildungs-Bataillon 253

LXXXI ARMEEKORPS – General der Infanterie Friedrich-August Schack

49. Infanterie Division – Generalleutnant Vollrath Lübbe
Divisions-Füsilier-Bataillon 149
Grenadier-Regiment 148 – Oberstlt Heinrich Klose
Grenadier-Regiment 149
Grenadier-Regiment 150
Artillerie-Regiment 149
275. Infanterie Division – Generalleutnant Hans Schmidt
Divisions-Füsilier-Bataillon 275
Grenadier-Regiment 983
Grenadier-Regiment 984
Grenadier-Regiment 985
Artillerie-Regiment 275
353. Infanterie Division* – Generalleutnant Paul Mahlmann
Divisions-Füsilier-Bataillon 353

Grenadier-Regiment 941 – Oberst Alexius Schmitz
Grenadier-Regiment 942 – Oberstleutnant Friedrich Tröster
Grenadier-Regiment 943 – Hauptmann Schindler
Panzerjäger-Abteilung 353
Pionier-Bataillon 353
Artillerie-Regiment 353
* Subordinated to LXXXVIII Armeekorps but rushed to the Aachen sector to bolster the defense.

9. Panzer Division – Generalleutnant Harald, Freiherr von Elverfeldt

Panzer-Regiment 33 – Oberst Ludwig Schmahl
Panzergrenadier-Regiment 10 – Oberstleutnant Dr. Johann Reich
Panzergrenadier-Regiment 11 – Oberst Maximilian Sperling
Panzerartillerie-Regiment 102
Panzeraufklärungs-Abteilung 9
Flak-Bataillon 287
Panzerjäger-Abteilung 50
Panzerpionier-Bataillon 86
105. Panzer-Brigade – Major Volker

116. Panzer Division – General der Panzertruppen Gerhard, Graf von Schwerin*

Panzer-Regiment 16 – Oberstleutnant Hans-Georg Lüder
Panzergrenadier-Regiment 60 – Oberstleutnant Helmut Zander
Panzergrenadier-Regiment 156 – Oberst Heinrich Voigtsberger
Panzerartillerie-Regiment 146 – Oberst Ernst Pean
Panzeraufklärungs-Abteilung 116 – Major Eberhard Stephan
Flak-Bataillon 281
Panzerjäger-Abteilung 226

Panzerpionier-Bataillon 675
* Replaced by Oberst Heinrich Voigtsberger on September 14, 1944, as interim commander, being officially replaced on September 20, 1944, by Oberst Siegfried von Waldenburg.

PRINCIPAL GERMAN REINFORCEMENTS

12. Infanterie (later Volksgrenadier) Division* – Oberst Gerhard Engel

Divisions-Füsilier-Bataillon 12
Grenadier-Regiment 48 – Oberstleutnant Wilhelm Osterhold
Grenadier-Regiment 89 – Oberstleutnant Gerhard Lemcke
Artillerie-Regiment 12 – Oberstleutnant Erwin Böhm
* Subordinated to LXXXI Armeekorps.

183. Volksgrenadier Division* – Generalleutnant Wolfgang Lange

Grenadier-Regiment 330 – Oberst Hampfner
Grenadier-Regiment 343 – Oberstleutnant Marchlewski
Grenadier-Regiment 351 – Oberst Dr. Schüder
Artillerie-Regiment 219 – Oberst Meyer
* Subordinated to II SS-Panzerkorps but deployed in the Aachen sector.

246. Volksgrenadier Division* – Oberst Gerhard Wilck

Grenadier-Regiment 352 – Oberstleutnant Josef Eggerstorfer
Grenadier-Regiment 404 – Major Wolf-Dieter Heimann
Grenadier-Regiment 689 – Oberstleutnant Maximilian Leyherr (ex-Kampfkommandant Aachen)
Artillerie-Regiment 246 – Oberst Schiele
* Subordinated to LXXXI Armeekorps, deployed as Aachen garrison.

OPPOSING PLANS

AMERICAN

With the senior commanders now able to see the damage wrought upon the enemy forces first hand – Eisenhower famously describing the scenes around Falaise as being a carpet of dead bodies and destroyed vehicles – the main effect of the Allied victory in France was to generate a false optimism about the capabilities of the German armed forces for the further prosecution of hostilities. The main obstacle now to a successful invasion of Germany proper was the Westwall – or "Western Rampart" – more commonly known to the Western Allies as the Siegfried Line.

It was against this backdrop that the staff of Montgomery's 21st Army Group developed a plan that, rather than engage the Westwall head on, would actually outflank the German defensive belt and offer egress into the enemy's industrial heartland – the Ruhr.

Codenamed *Market Garden*, the plan was to use airborne troops to seize a number of bridges across the rivers Meuse (Maas), Waal, and Rhine, with these forces to be quickly relieved by an armored thrust that would smash

American armor taking a moment's respite near the burning wreckage of a German Sd.Kfz. 251 half-track.

through the German lines and consolidate the position at the final bridge at Arnhem, creating a bridgehead on the eastern bank of the Rhine from where an attack into Germany proper could be launched.

The implementation of this plan naturally meant that it would be prioritized for logistical support, and thus the instructions to Bradley's 12th Army Group would be for the First and Third Armies (to be later joined by the Ninth) to continue their eastwards advance to the Rhine where they would also attempt to secure crossing points at places such as Bonn or Cologne, the latter having the distinction of being one of the largest rail hubs in the western part of Germany. The only real strategic concession made was that the city of Aachen would ultimately form the boundary between First and Ninth Armies and rather than incur costly losses in unnecessary street fighting, the city would initially be bypassed and its defenders allowed to wither on the vine, being mopped up by supporting formations.

In effect, Hodges' plan was a simple advance on a broad front, trusting that superiority in all branches of service would suffice to ensure that each of his three corps would reach their objectives, and few if any on the Allied staffs paid detailed attention to a relatively small area of wooded hills– shown on their maps as the Hürtgenwald – which lay some 15km (10 miles), to the southeast of Aachen. After initial – limited – contacts, Hodges' command had the opportunity to simply bypass the forest and have the troops move directly on the plain around Zülpich and from there to an area between Cologne and Bonn, as had been the plan with Aachen itself, but instead it was decided that the forest should be first cleared of enemy troops.

It was a decision which would have incalculable ramifications and one from which, having committed itself, the US First Army would find it both mentally and physically difficult to disengage itself, with plans and objectives changing on an almost daily basis. It was a situation that the military historian, Russell F. Weigley, openly questioned when he commented that, "The most likely way to make the Hürtgen a menace to the American army was to send American troops attacking into its depths. An army that depends for its superiority on its mobility, firepower and technology should never voluntarily give battle where these assets are at a discount: the Hürtgen Forest was surely such a place."

GERMAN

As August drew to a close, and never one to sugarcoat a bad situation, Model had literally bombarded his superiors with a series of reports about the military situation in the west.

Of perhaps the most immediate import was his opinion that the Westwall itself had been a "vanity project" and that, as a strategic defense, it was no longer "fit for purpose" – indeed, just by saying this, Model was more or less reiterating earlier comments made by both Alfred Jodl and Gerd von Rundstedt who had referred to the installations as being "little more than a building site" and "woefully inadequate," respectively.

Unlike the Maginot Line, the German fortifications were a combination of several distinct building projects undertaken during the late 1930s, which meant that although the defenses in some sectors were fairly comprehensive, in others they were almost non-existent, creating gaps through which enemy troops could penetrate almost at will. In addition to this, the German victory in 1940 had meant that the original purpose of the fortification had become obsolete and thus much of its fixtures, fittings, and impedimenta had either been removed and repurposed for use in the Atlantikwall or had simply been appropriated by the local population. Finally, much of the construction had become dilapidated and needed updating or replacement.

In conference (left to right): Generalfeldmarschall Model (OB Heeresgruppe B), Generalfeldmarschall von Rundstedt (OB West), and General Hans Krebs (CoS, Heeresgruppe B). (Bundesarchiv, Bild 146-1978-024-31/ CC BY-SA 3.0 DE https:// creativecommons.org/licenses/ by-sa/3.0/de/deed.en, via Wikimedia Commons)

To that end, Model had stipulated that without a significant overhaul of the Westwall, a successful defense of Germany's western border would be impossible. He therefore requested urgent action on national and local levels which would require the deployment of construction workers from agencies such as the Organisation Todt (OT) and Reichsarbeitsdienst (Reich Labor Service or RAD) as well as resources drawn from the Fortress Pioneer Staffs of the V (Stuttgart), VI (Münster), and XII (Wiesbaden) Military Districts – the former to repair and upgrade the bunker and entrenchment systems, with the latter also being responsible for the extension of existing and laying of new minefields.

It is unclear that if another officer, of whatever rank, had voiced such an opinion it would have received a similar reception, but on August 24, Hitler gave instructions for Model's request to be complied with in full, and then gave further orders that some 200,000 forced laborers be taken from prisons, POW camps, or concentration camps to supplement the available manpower.

When it came to the forces remaining under arms, Model was obliged to advise OKW that during the Normandy Campaign his command had suffered an estimated 400,000 casualties – approximately 30,000 dead, 83,000 wounded, and 295,000 either captured or missing in action, together with a further 95,000 trapped behind the front lines in isolated garrisons and whose sole future contribution to the campaign would be to tie up as many enemy troops as possible before their inevitable capitulation. Of these, it was the number of troops whose fate was unaccounted for that naturally caused the greatest ground for uncertainty for, in continuing his report in such a manner that its contents would be sure to reach the ears of the Führer, Model now enumerated that the combined strength of the principal forces under his command – the 7. and 15. Armees – amounted to no more than the equivalent of a single reduced strength Panzer division and a further six infantry divisions of varying size and effectiveness.

As an example of the attrition that had been suffered by Model's troops, the divisional history of the "Hitlerjugend" states that it arrived in Normandy slightly above official strength, but that when the remnants of the division crossed the Franco-Belgian border at the beginning of September, it could muster no more than three weak grenadier battalions of 150–200 men each, two pioneer platoons, one Sd.Kfz. 124 Wespe, a composite battery of three light and two heavy field pieces, a battery of ten Nebelwerfer, one 75mm Pak 40 antitank gun, and a single 88mm Flak 41 anti-aircraft gun.

In time, Model remained confident that many of the missing troops would find their way back to German lines and return to duty, but until then he would have to contain an enemy force estimated as being in the region of 54 divisions. It was not only a force that could punch through the porous German lines with ease but one that could also be quickly reinforced by the significant number of troops OKW believed were already stationed in Great Britain and merely awaiting suitable weather conditions and the availability of sufficient lift capacity before being deployed on the Continent.

His first – and indeed only – priority was to stabilize the German *Hauptkampflinie* (front line, HKL). Once this had been achieved, the troops could be reorganized, reinforced, and resupplied, but to do this, the withdrawal needed to be stopped and the troops placed in some semblance of order.

As intended, Model's report had a sobering effect on both his military and political superiors and in early September he would be given the welcome news that Student's 1. Fallschirm-Armee (1st Parachute Army) and Bittrich's II SS-Panzerkorps would be attached to his army group. On paper, at least, this was a significant reinforcement, one which would enable Model to deploy both the 7. and 15. Armees in a more concentrated fashion, but nonetheless the two formations were far from being combat ready – the 1. Fallschirm-Armee, for example, was an amalgam of units that had been badly mauled during the fighting in Normandy organized into a composite formation that owed its grandiose designation to its designated commander's exalted rank in the Luftwaffe. On the other hand, the 9. and 10. SS-Panzer Divisions ("Hohenstaufen" and "Frundsberg") that formed Bittrich's command were both veteran formations which, after suffering heavy losses in the recent campaign, had been withdrawn to the Netherlands to rest and refit.

In order to both facilitate the construction work on the Westwall and to rotate and reorganize his forces, Model's only recourse was to attempt to trade space for time, delaying the enemy advance long enough to stabilize the front line and integrate any replacements or reinforcements as and when they were released by OKW. In this, he knew that he would be aided by delays caused by both the logistical bottleneck arising from the increasing distance between the Allied spearheads and their logistical hubs as well as what would seem in retrospect to have been an overemphasis in the Allied higher command echelons on the sacrosanctity of formation boundaries, which had been seen on occasion to have held a greater importance than finding and defeating the enemy.

An M10 "Wolverine" tank destroyer supporting US infantry during house-to-house fighting.

As a result, Model subsequently gave orders on August 31 for the establishment of a defensive line stretching from Antwerp southwards through Louvain and Namur, skirting the city of Luxembourg before ending at Toul in eastern France. The principal positions were to be manned by September 4, with the remainder of the troops scheduled to be in position before the 15th of the month, the whole forming the forward defense that Model intended to act as a buffer between the Allies and the engineering work progressing in his rear areas.

The German Sturmgewehr 44 was perhaps the world's first assault rifle. (Armémuseum [The Swedish Army Museum], CC BY-SA 4.0 https:// creativecommons. org/licenses/by-sa/4.0, via Wikimedia Commons)

In addition, and in due consideration of the enemy's almost complete air superiority and air landing capacity, Model now advised OKW of his intention to relocate his headquarters closer to the German border.

The following day, and in consideration of the increasing pressure that Model would soon be facing both as an army group commander and indeed a front commander, the Führer again intervened, announcing that the two roles would again be split and that while Model would retain command of Heeresgruppe B, the position of OB West would once again be assumed by Generalfeldmarschall Gerd von Rundstedt. With this higher command now taken from him, Model was able to review and rationalize the state of the troops under his command to prepare them for combat at the earliest instance.

To that end, OKW advised Rundstedt that OB West would receive – for defensive purposes – a reinforcement of some 30 independent fortress battalions which would be later increased by additional troops throughout the month. Furthermore, and within a separate time frame, other infantry and armored formations would be transferred to the Western Front once they had completed their refitting within the borders of the Reich. While welcome in itself, an ominous codicil to this news was that the Army High Command could not commit to nor guarantee later reinforcement until such time as the situations on other fronts had clarified themselves.

This would mean that Model would now need to lobby Rundstedt for much-needed reinforcements, the task being made slightly easier by the recent allocation of the 5. Panzerarmee to Blaskowitz' Heeresgruppe G. In addition, he had to devise two operational plans, one for each of his proposed defensive positions. The first of these would naturally be to hold the Antwerp–Toul line for as long as possible while maintaining what, given the meager resources available to him, would be a limited mobile reserve to counter any sudden enemy breakthrough. The second plan would also be defensive in nature but would be pinned upon the refurbished Westwall with the upgraded defenses facilitating the establishment of an adequate reserve for the purpose of limited counterattacks.

Without waiting for Rundstedt to respond to his "request," Model continued with the process of rationalization. It was a bold decision, and one which precluded the creation of a dedicated tactical reserve, instead relying on corps commanders to juggle their resources as best they could. A risky strategy, it seemingly surrendered the initiative to the enemy, but having studied the Allies' progress across northern Europe, Model was confident that if he could simply parry the enemy thrusts, even for a matter of days, he would gain enough time not only to reorganize his forces but also for a deterioration in the weather to deny the enemy their hitherto unassailable advantages of mobility, firepower, and airpower.

THE CAMPAIGN

FROM NORMANDY TO VICTORY

Although they had been rightly hailed as victories, the recent Allied successes, together with the subsequent German withdrawal, had themselves served to create a series of problems that now threatened to simply overwhelm Allied logistical capabilities and stop the advance dead in its tracks. With their leading elements moving increasingly farther from the landing beaches, and in the absence of a fully functioning supply system, the Allied commissariat was obliged to implement a system of unit prioritization, a case of "robbing Peter to pay Paul" on a grand scale.

Given these restrictions, Eisenhower's staff at SHAEF (Supreme Headquarters Allied Expeditionary Force) was faced with having to follow one of two possible courses of action. The first was to either slow down, or even halt, the advance in order to give the supply trains the time needed to catch up with the units they were supporting and thereby ease the supply problem. The second was to accept the risk and simply continue the advance at its current tempo, pressing the retreating Germans as hard as possible in order to prevent them from being able to reorganize or to be reinforced from within Germany or the occupied territories.

In his narrative *Crusade in Europe*, Eisenhower describes the situation as follows:

> ... A reinforced division, in active operations, consumes from 600 to 700 tons of supplies per day. When battling in a fixed position, most of this tonnage is represented in ammunition; on the march the bulk is devoted to petrol and lubricants ... With thirty-six divisions in action we were faced with the problem of delivering from beaches and ports to the front lines some 20,000 tons of supplies every day. Our spearheads, moreover, were moving swiftly, frequently seventy-five miles per day. The supply service had to catch these with loaded trucks. Every mile of advance doubled the difficulty because the supply truck had always to make a two-way run from the beaches and back in order to deliver another load to the marching troops. Other thousands of tons had to go into advanced airfields for construction and subsequent maintenance. Still additional amounts were required for the repair of bridges and roads for which heavy equipment was necessary.

Given this, and with the numerical equivalent of an estimated dozen or so full-strength enemy divisions still standing between the Allied front lines and the German border, the Supreme Commander continued by saying:

> When the action is proceeding as rapidly as it did across France during the hectic days of late August and early September every commander from division upward becomes obsessed with the idea that with only a few more tons of supply he could rush right on and win the war. This is the spirit that wins wars and is always to be encouraged. Initiative, confidence and boldness are among the most admirable traits of a good combat leader. As we dashed across France and Belgium each commander, therefore, begged and demanded priority over all others and it was undeniable that in front of each were the opportunities for quick exploitation that made the demands completely logical.

Like beaters driving game into the guns of waiting hunters, Eisenhower had decided, much to the chagrin of certain of his principal subordinates, to continue with his preferred broad-front strategy, his plan being to avoid a direct head-on collision with enemy forces, and instead achieve success by maneuver, forcing them to give ground or face encirclement. As he stated in his book, the intention being for the Allies to "… keep the Germans guessing as to the direction of our main thrust, cause them to extend their forces and by doing so leave them open to defeat in detail."

The question that Eisenhower asked himself was naturally how this objective could best be achieved, and, in effect, his plan was that each of the two subordinate formations under his command would make a separate drive for the Rhine. Being the closest of the two in terms of distance from the Channel Coast and the crucially important air support from bases in England, Montgomery's 21st Army Group would drive straight west in a line that would bypass Aachen, reaching the Rhine somewhere north of Cologne. For its part, Bradley's 12th US Army Group was to move towards the Upper Rhine near the city of Metz from where it would presumably conduct joint operations with Devers' 6th Army Group, then moving up through southern France. That this plan never came to fruition was simply due to the fortunes of war that saw the creation of a second "pocket" of German troops near to the Belgian city of Mons and the redeployment of Collins' VII Corps northeastwards from First Army's right flank into a blocking position east of the city in an attempt to complete the encirclement and, by blocking the enemy line of retreat, force their surrender.

Militarily, and by the time that this operation had concluded on September 5, it could be considered a proven success in that a further 25,000 Germans had been captured. But operationally, it necessitated a realignment of the Allied armies themselves so that Aachen now fell within First Army's operational zone and that the two axes of advance that Eisenhower had originally envisaged had potentially morphed into three, with Montgomery's troops being edged northwards and establishing the conditions for perhaps the most ambitious airborne operation in history.

On Thursday August 31, Omar Bradley flew to First Army's headquarters in order to discuss with Hodges his intentions for the next stage of the campaign, which were to continue with Eisenhower's "broad front" strategy with Hodges' troops advancing on a northwest axis at "best possible speed," their movement being aided by what Bradley named Operation *Linnet*, a

A US soldier posing by the side of a wrecked German JgdPz 38(t) "Hetzer" tank destroyer. Based upon a Czech tank chassis, these small vehicles nonetheless "punched above their weight," mounting a 75mm Pak 39 L/48 gun.

series of airborne landings to secure the city of Tournai and its crossings over the river Schelde, which were scheduled to be made three days later on September 3. Hodges immediately directed his corps commanders to comply with these instructions but, while the requisite progress was more or less made, *Linnet* was aborted at the last moment as Tournai had been captured by elements of the British XXX Corps before the transports had even left the ground.

Given the state of preparedness of the airborne troops, Bradley then tabled the possibility of a second landing – *Linnet II* – which would take place the following day. This revised operation was now intended to capture both the Maastricht Triangle and a number of bridges over the river Maas which lay directly in front of First Army's advance, thus paving the way for a continued movement to render Model's improvised defensive line more or less untenable.

But just like its namesake, *Linnet II* was also destined to remain firmly on the ground when, on September 10, fate, in the form of Britain's Field Marshal Sir Bernard Montgomery, intervened. Montgomery saw a greater potential for the concept exhibited in both the *Linnet* operations, and went directly to the Supreme Commander with a more audacious plan, codenamed *Market Garden*. It would use a carpet of airborne troops to seize several bridges and crossing points across the rivers Maas and Waal before seizing the vital Rijnbrug (Rhine Bridge) at Arnhem, and in so doing give the Allies a viable bridgehead on the eastern bank of the Rhine. In its author's own words, the plan had the clear potential to shorten the war in Europe and by doing so reduce the total of future Allied casualties, and it was no doubt this last consideration that caused Eisenhower to give it his assent. While Montgomery produced a detailed and viable operational plan, Bradley issued orders of his own, effectively telling Hodges and Patton – his two army commanders – to push ahead regardless, in the belief that a successful thrust would see American troops breaking through the German lines at one or more locations between

Cologne in the north and Saarbrücken in the south prior to forcing a passage across the Rhine.

But even if Montgomery's claims could indeed be realized, Eisenhower still remained acutely aware that his decision would place an inordinate strain upon the Allies' logistical capacity: without access to a functioning deepwater port, every barrel of fuel, every box of ammunition, every crate of food allocated to the proposed attack would mean less of each commodity that could be allocated to the forces under Bradley's command. Whatever his personal relationships with his warring subordinates, the Supreme Commander was pragmatic enough to realize that by extension Montgomery's plan would also give the Allies the best opportunity to capture Antwerp. In his estimation, should bad weather force the closure of the existing ports and harbors for more than even a few consecutive days, it would not only prove disastrous for the continued prosecution of the Allied offensive, but also for the movement of replacements and reinforcements to the front. In Brittany, for example, Simpson's Ninth Army was due to be transferred to the German border once it had secured the capture of the port of Brest, a movement that held its own logistical implications.

For Bradley, this meant that his two subordinates would need to carefully husband their resources in order for the advance to continue and the enemy be denied the opportunity to regroup his forces. It also meant that – in Hodges' eyes at least – Montgomery would be given priority access to the primary road network to move his ground forces to their start positions while the Americans would effectively be relegated to secondary and minor roads while still being expected to maintain pressure on the retreating Germans.

In order to cope with these changes in focus, Eisenhower decided that Montgomery would now adjust his axis of advance more to the northeast, while Bradley would continue his eastward advance. The idea being that Ninth Army – once it had completed its current assignment – would ultimately slot between them and provide support for both. Nonetheless,

Battery of US 155mm SP howitzers firing a "symbolic round" into German territory.

while this would represent a much-needed and welcome reinforcement, the logistics involved in transporting a whole army across the width of France would, in the current circumstances, serve only to place even further pressure upon an already strained transport infrastructure.

As Bradley's armies continued their push eastwards, a number of sharp encounters should have served to remind them that, despite all appearances, while the Wehrmacht might be in retreat it was nonetheless far from beaten. However, the overwhelming consensus remained that the enemy had neither the intent nor the facility to stand and hold their ground, and that the Allies successfully reaching the Rhine was nothing other than a foregone conclusion. It was an assumption that Hodges' staff in particular would soon come to be disabused of. After a series of small meeting engagements, reports were soon coming back stating that the terrain ahead was unconducive to a penetration in force.

HITTING THE WESTWALL

H-Hour was scheduled for the night of September 11/12, 1944, and although Hodges had authorized the forward movement to be a simple "reconnaissance in force," the term itself meant different things to his various corps commanders.

The southernmost of the First Army's three corps – V Corps under Leonard T. Gerow – had perhaps the most difficult of missions, ostensibly that of continuing the general advance while simultaneously maintaining the link with Patton's Third Army. Indeed, Gerow's orders were that his corps should act "in conjunction with Third Army" and as such compliance would have entailed his closing the gap between the two armies while at the same time increasing the operating distance between his men and Collins' VII Corps, thereby rendering his ability to fulfill Hodges' orders almost impossible.

In order to follow his orders, Gerow elected to place Maj. Gen. Lunsford Oliver's recently transferred 5th Armored Division on the right of his line, where its mobility would allow it to not only maintain contact with Patton's army but also to cover the extended gap which would be generated by the projected movement of the 4th and 28th Infantry Divisions as they continued their own advance. Gerow's decision, while it resolved all calls upon his corps, crucially emphasized one aspect of his armored force, that of speed and maneuverability, while simultaneously denying him the offensive power that such troops represented. His justification for this was that, as per Hodges' description, the

Detail of the Dragon's Teeth or *Panzersperren*, part of the Westwall defenses. (Ormonde Military History Society)

Acclaimed author Ernest Hemingway (right) "embedded" himself with the 22nd Infantry Regiment, commanded by his friend Col. Charles T. Lanham. Hemingway was not the only literary participant of the battle – J. D. Salinger and Kurt Vonnegut both saw service within American ranks.

coming operation would be just a reconnaissance, albeit one in force, with reinforced patrols being sent forward to gain updated intelligence about the enemy's defenses and deployments while much-needed supplies were brought forward in preparation for a later coordinated attack across the army's front. This would give him several days for this initial phase before going over to the offensive, with Oliver being instructed to hold one of his combat commands in readiness for immediate deployment in order to exploit any gains made by either of the infantry divisions. By way of compensation for this latter deployment, a regimental combat team – Lt. Col. Carl L. Peterson's 112th Infantry – was attached to the 5th Armored to provide Oliver some much-needed infantry support for close action.

Having latterly advanced through the Ardennes region of Belgium, the men of V Corps would most likely have thought themselves appreciative of the heavy woods, ravines, streams, and ridges that lay before them, as because of this arduous natural terrain the Germans had merely created a thinner belt of fixed defenses there. However, those that they had built were placed in a concentrated fashion to cover those approach routes which their engineers had determined to be the most likely for the Americans to use for their advance.

Situated close to the boundary with VII Corps, the 4th and 28th Infantry Divisions were ordered to push northeastwards across a series of successive ridgelines with the intention of bringing them through the rugged highlands into a position near the valley of the Mosel from where they could drive farther east to the city of Koblenz, where the latter waterway flowed into the Rhine. As such, Gerow's intent was to continue the style of pursuit that had taken his troops to the German border, with no real consideration for a possible concentration of forces in the face of the enemy. At this time, V Corps occupied an approximate frontage of roughly 50km (30 miles), whereby the infantry covered a little under half of the distance, with the armor covering the rest. As such, Gerow's deployment was eminently suitable for the intelligence reports that he

Troops of the 1st Infantry
Division with captured
VW Kübelwagen (Type 82).

Troops of the 1st Infantry Division with captured VW Kübelwagen (Type 82).

received via his G-2, Col. Thomas J. Ford, who informed him that, at best, V Corps was still facing the battered remnants of the same three enemy divisions that it had been pursuing for the last several weeks and that there was no real reason to radically change this estimation, adding that, "There seems no doubt that the enemy will defend [the Siegfried Line] with all of the forces that he can gather, but what those forces will be is open to question."

Gerow's task was to be made easier by the fact that his axis of advance would not only hit the enemy lines on the boundary between two enemy corps, but also those of their parent formations – Brandenberger's 7. Armee and Knobelsdorff's 1. Armee, from Heeresgruppen B and G, respectively. For the enemy to react coherently, it would oblige the Germans to exhibit a significant degree of mutual communication and cooperation between formations at several levels, but as an example and given the prevalent opinion at First Army's Headquarters with regard to the enemy's capacity for combat, Hodges' own G-2, Col. Benjamin A. Dickson, advised his commanding officer, "At the present time, LXXXI Corps cannot hold a defense line with these forces ..."

If Dickson's appraisal of the strategic situation was correct, then the most apposite area of deployment for Gerow's armored troops – or at least Oliver's reaction force – would have been in this northern sector. Instead, it was as far from this point as it could reasonably be expected to be. Moreover, the situation was far more nuanced than the Americans had either believed or anticipated. Again, and because of their experiences in Russia, the Germans had adopted a well-rehearsed tactic by which – when attacked – the forward defense line would slowly collapse in on itself and occupy a refurbished Westwall in conjunction with both locally organized forces and other reinforcements transferred from within Germany proper. The tactic was to prove a success, as American supply problems afforded the Germans the time necessary to withdraw into their second line of defensive positions. By the same token, however, it only gave Rundstedt – as OB West – a mere two of

US V Corps operations, September 11–19, 1944

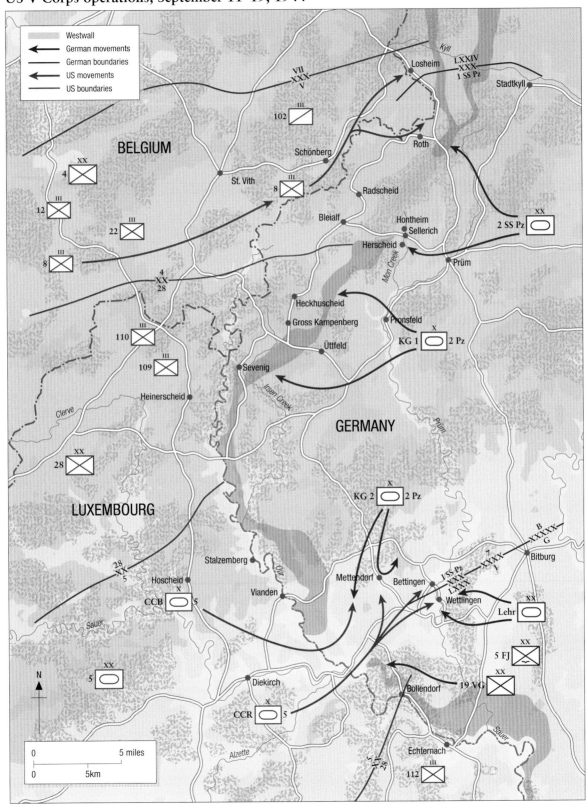

Legend:
- Westwall
- German movements
- German boundaries
- US movements
- US boundaries

BELGIUM

GERMANY

LUXEMBOURG

Losheim · Kyll · Stadtkyll

LXXIV
XXX
1 SS Pz

VII
XXX
V

102 (III)

Schönberg · Roth

St. Vith · 8 (III) · Radscheid

4 (XX) · 12 (III) · 22 (III) · 8 (III)

Bleialf · Hontheim · Sellerich

Herscheid · 2 SS Pz (XX)

Mont Creek · Prüm

4
XX
28

Heckhuscheid

Gross Kampenberg · Pronsfeld

Üttfeld · KG 1 (X) 2 Pz

110 (III) · 109 (III)

Sevenig · Irsen Creek

Heinerscheid

Clerve

28 (XX)

KG 2 (X) 2 Pz

28
XX
5

Stalzemberg · Our · Prüm

B
XXXXX
G

7
XXXX · Bitburg

Hoscheid · Mettendorf · Bettingen

I SS Pz
XXX
LXXX

CCB (X) 5 · Vianden · Wettlingen · Lehr (XX)

5 (XX)

Sauer

Diekirch · 5 FJ (XX)

CCR (X) 5 · Bollendorf · 19 VG (XX)

N

Alzette · Echternach · 112 (III)

5
XX
28

Sauer

```
0                    5 miles
0        5km
```

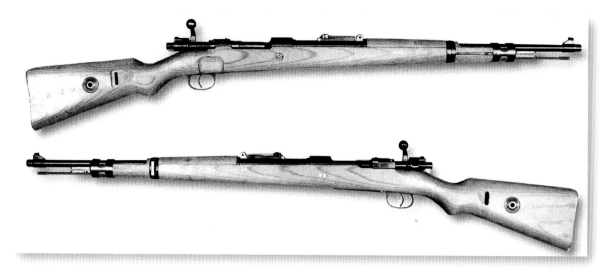

The standard German infantry weapon was the Mauser Karabiner 98k(urz) (7.62mm cal). (Armémuseum [The Swedish Army Museum], CC BY-SA 3.0 https://creativecommons.org/licenses/by-sa/3.0, via Wikimedia Commons)

the six weeks that he had informed Berlin that he required in order to mount a feasible defense along the Westwall.

Given the meandering nature of the German–Belgian border, the first of the V Corps units to encounter the enemy was actually the farthest to the west, the 28th Infantry Division under Brig. Gen. Norman D. Cota, whose forces initially moved southeast onto the Schnee Eifel, preceded by strong patrols sent ahead into enemy territory in order to seize terrain, which they would hold until these gains were consolidated during the hours of darkness as the rest of the division moved up. The whole process was repeated on the following day, and then the day after that, until they reached the German border near the town of Üttfeld.

The physical invasion of Germany began neither against a backdrop of artillery nor a hail of small arms fire. Instead, and far less glamorously, it took place amid an atmosphere of confusion when, at 0815hrs on the morning of September 11, 1944, Maj. Gen. William B. Kean, Hodges' Chief of Staff, advised him that a report had been received to the effect that elements of the 5th US Armored Division[2] had crossed the border into enemy territory. Hodges immediately called Gerow to confirm the substance of the report, only to be told that the corps commander had no knowledge of the matter whatsoever. As the day progressed, it soon became clear that further patrols had also crossed the border. In physical terms, these were nothing more than a minor encroachment and while there were no claims or fanfares proclaiming that the Siegfried Line had been breached, the fact was that – however small it might be – a small part of Hitler's Germany was now under American occupation. Despite this delay in confirmation, it was not to be long before Hodges received the news he had been hoping for when, on the afternoon of September 12, advance elements of VII Corps had not only crossed into Germany but would later engage the enemy in a short – if one-sided – firefight.

First Army's war diary would later record that the first official encounter between American and German troops would take place shortly after

2   It would later be confirmed that the patrol in question was from the 2nd Platoon, B Company, 85th Cavalry Reconnaissance Squadron (mech), 5th Armored Division: Sgt, Warner W. Holzinger, Cpl Ralph E. Diven, Cpl (T5) T. Locke, Pfc William McColligan, George F. McNeal, and Jesse Stephens together with a French officer, Lt Lionel DeLille, who was acting as interpreter. Having crossed the border near Keppeshausen, the men reconnoitered several unoccupied pillboxes near Waldhof before safely withdrawing to their own lines without having encountered any enemy troops.

1515hrs on Tuesday September 12, between troops from Charlie Company, 1st Battalion, 16th Infantry and an unspecified enemy unit. It would, however, ultimately be a different encounter between a VII Corps unit and the German defenders which would grab the newspaper headlines.

Cota's advance against the German positions almost immediately became a lesson in improvisation, as it was soon blatantly obvious that the 28th Infantry Division was singularly ill-equipped for the objectives it had been given. The nature of First Army's advance and the preconceptions it had generated amongst its officer corps had meant that, even taking into account the known supply problems, no provision had been made to provide the troops with specialist equipment such as flamethrowers or explosive charges for use against enemy pillboxes or bunkers. With many of the tanks and self-propelled tank destroyers having been taken out of the line for repair and refit, local artillery support was limited to a small number of antitank guns and towed tank destroyers, while the infantrymen themselves had little enough small arms ammunition with which to conduct anything other than a cursory engagement.

On top of this, and again given supply restrictions, Cota's artillery – the one branch of service that all later commentators would consistently describe as having performed to the best of its capability – was shackled by a directive from 28th Division's HQ that explicitly forbade any form of engagement apart from either pre-registered targets or fire missions that had been expressly approved by divisional headquarters. In addition, and presumably to conserve ammunition, each of Cota's regiments – the 109th and 110th infantry – were permitted to commit only a single battalion into action at any one time.

When the attacking troops came up against the German defenses on September 13, they were simply outgunned and outclassed by an enemy firing on them from prepared positions, and when towed guns were brought forward to give close fire support, their crews were simply shot down as they tried to bring their weapons into action. The following day, and

Troops of the 1st Infantry Division move forward cautiously in advance of their armored support.

43

Waiting for orders – men of the 28th Infantry Division in a final briefing.

having learned the hard way, Cota removed all previous restrictions and even rushed forward several armored vehicles that had completed their repairs. Although these measures added impetus to the American advance it still meant that as the troops pushed farther into the defensive belt, they did so without adequate support weapons and equipment, only to find themselves caught in a confusing maze of minefields, barbed wire, and antitank defenses.

Months earlier, during the D-Day landings, Cota had shown calculated aggression when he led a grenade attack against a German strongpoint that was holding up the advance. Now he showed the same uncompromising determination to succeed when he relieved Col. William L. Blanton from command of the 109th Infantry on the grounds that one of the regiment's battalions had executed an unauthorized withdrawal, which had – to Cota's mind – compromised the success of the division's attack.

In a succession of bloody encounters, American casualties were inordinately high. So much so that, taking their cue from the 28th's divisional insignia of a red keystone, the German defenders started referring to their erstwhile opponents as "*die Männer des blutigen Eimers*" or "the men of the Bloody Bucket." It was a badge of honor that would be earned again and again during the coming fighting.

Eventually, Cota's regiments were close enough to be able to use point-blank high-explosive fire to batter their way through the enemy defenses and, while their territorial gains were meager, they soon had a far greater prize: intelligence reports from captured enemy soldiers providing them with a far clearer picture of the situation to their front. Many bunkers and pillboxes having but a skeleton garrison while others – as Sgt Holzinger's patrol could testify – were simply unmanned and thus defensively redundant.

For the next two days, casualties mounted as the American regiments beat their way forward. However, even as they reached their high water mark on September 15, a nighttime German counterattack in platoon strength supported by two half-tracks equipped with improvised flamethrowers recaptured a position that had been taken several hours earlier by Fox Company of the 110th Infantry and threatened to cancel much of that day's gains. The following day, the US troops renewed their attack and again their efforts were rewarded with success, particularly in the sector occupied by the regiment's 1st Battalion, where they were able to break through the Westwall into the open countryside beyond.

With the troops under his command standing on the verge of a possible breakthrough, it was with mixed emotions that the divisional commander greeted Gerow on the afternoon of September 16, the commanding general having arrived at Cota's headquarters to personally inform him that, with the division's two lead regiments having taken something in excess of 1,500 casualties in such a short but intensive period of combat, he was calling off the attack pending reinforcement and resupply. Intermittent low-intensity fighting continued to take place over the following days, but to all intents and purposes, the 28th Infantry Division's role in the Battle of the Borders was temporarily at an end.

To the north, and as 28th Division began its move southeastwards, its "running mate," the 4th Infantry Division, began its own drive to the northeast. Unsure of what lay to his front, the divisional commander, Maj. Gen. Raymond O. Barton, was more conservative than Cota had been but nonetheless his regiments made good time, arriving into their attack positions during September 13, in time to comply with Gerow's timetable of attack, which was set for the following day. The inevitable problem was that every yard of ground gained would then increase the distance between the two American divisions.

Adverse terrain and a heavy drizzle combined to delay the two regiments – 12th and 22nd Infantry – that Barton had committed to the operation and his attack went in piecemeal, exactly as had Cota's. The difference was, that while the 28th had encountered manned defensive works, Barton's troops quickly found, to their surprise, that most of the bunkers and pillboxes to their front were unoccupied, enemy resistance being so slight that only one or two fire missions were requested from the divisional artillery. This is not to say that the 4th Division was to encounter no opposition whatsoever – as elements of the 22nd Infantry approached the road junction near Bleialf, there was a sharp report and the leading tank burst into flames, victim of a concealed 88mm gun. Confusion reigned as the remaining vehicles took evasive action, but eventually order was restored and – reasoning that the greatest protection would be to close with the enemy – the GIs elected to advance at the run, their charge carrying them into and then through the German positions. As the supporting units moved up behind them to police the battlefield and secure prisoners, Col. Charles T. Lanham, commanding the 22nd Infantry, threw the remainder of his regiment into the action, resulting in a much-needed success. Lanham's men created a two-mile wide breach in the Westwall, penetrating a similar distance into the German rear.

Throughout the night of September 14, and while Barton's men took measures to consolidate their position, German attempts to organize a counterattack failed due to a lack of available troops. Even with the inclusion of late reinforcements, SS-Brigadeführer Heinz Lammerding was able to pull together only a scratch force of less than 3,000 men with limited armored and artillery support – which he then decided would have had little or no chance in a frontal attack against a now-prepared enemy. Despite Cota's travails that day, Barton's success convinced both Gerow and indeed Barton himself that the path towards the Rhine now lay open before them.

But fate is said to be a fickle mistress, and despite the optimism felt at V Corps Headquarters, the situation began to slowly tilt in favor of the defenders. Hoping to widen the breach in the enemy lines and achieve a decisive breakthrough, Barton now committed his reserve – the 8th Infantry – to the battle, but the maneuver failed when the troops ran straight into a series of roadblocks and destroyed bridges that impeded the advance and

American stretcher parties evacuate casualties during a lull in the fighting.

then a heavy mist fell, effectively grounding the aircraft that Barton had been relying on to provide his men with tactical air support. Unperturbed, Col. James S. Rodwell of the 8th continued to press on with his assignment but, by late afternoon, after his attack had simply run out of steam, he advised the divisional commander that he would reorganize his regiment during the hours of darkness, intending to resume the attack at first light the following morning.

His confidence possibly undermined by the suddenness of this reverse, Barton now received news of enemy activity in the sectors occupied by his other two regiments, with both units reporting a sharp increase in enemy artillery fire, coupled with a number of attempts by the Germans to infiltrate the gaps in the American front lines. Further progress across the divisional frontage was slow but steady, measured in short advances leading to periods of stabilization and consolidation before the next phase of the advance began, and on September 17 the dynamic of V Corps' operations changed when it was announced that Gerow had been temporarily relieved of command and replaced by Maj. Gen. Albert H. Brooks, commander of the 2nd Armored Division.

The reason for this abrupt change in command was that Gerow had been summoned back to Washington to testify before an Army Board investigating the causes behind America's failure to anticipate the Japanese attack on Pearl Harbor. Gerow would ultimately return to the corps command after the hearing had closed, but he would be absent from the front at possibly the most crucial part of the campaign.

Brooks' appointment was, initially at least, merely the appointment of a "safe pair of hands" to oversee the corps' activities during Gerow's absence, with his departure effectively signaling the end of V Corps' involvement in the initial phase of the campaign. Hodges had been particularly wary of a gap opening up between First and Third Armies on one hand and then between V and VII Corps on the other, hence the earlier release of much-needed fuel to Gerow, which could arguably have been best used by Hodges' main thrust. That said, V Corps' limited successes in the early days of the campaign had undoubtedly served to polarize German attention so that adequate forces needed to be maintained in position in order to counter the latent threat posed by Gerow's troops, who, although their attack had temporarily ground to a halt, would ultimately be capable of further offensive action once their losses had been replaced and their supplies replenished.

For the time being, the men of the "Bloody Bucket" would maintain their position but events in the VII Corps sector, and a radical change in First Army's campaign objectives, would soon require their participation in some of the hardest and bloodiest fighting of the European Campaign.

"LIGHTNING JOE"

When the time came for Hodges to give orders for his "reconnaissance" towards the Rhine, it was hardly happenstance that Joseph L. Collins – arguably his most able subordinate – would be tasked with the principal role in the coming operation. All of First Army's corps commanders were proven and competent officers but it was Collins' recent performance in Normandy facilitating both the breakout from the beachhead and the capture of Cherbourg and the Cotentin Peninsula which had further raised his stock amongst his peers and senior officers, something which would ultimately lead Bradley to form the opinion that – in time – Collins would be worthy of an army command.

VII Corps' role would therefore be to drive through the area south of Aachen towards the Rhine, sweeping through the northern part of the Hürtgenwald with infantry while its armor pushed through a narrow strip of open land between the city and the forest, which would later become known as the "Stolberg Corridor." In the event, and perhaps mindful of Hodges' earlier instructions with regard to the expenditure of fuel and ammunition, Collins revised his original plan and instead instructed Maj. Gen. Clarence R. Huebner, commander of the 1st Infantry Division – "The Big Red One" – to probe towards the southern flank of Aachen with elements of two infantry regiments[3] – the 16th and 18th – while his third regiment, the 26th, would remain as a combat reserve. In a mutually supporting role, the 3rd Armored Division was then ordered to push into the forest and seek out a route that would enable VII Corps to bypass Aachen to the south, allowing it to push ahead into the open terrain beyond the city in preparation for the next stage of the operation. The remainder of Huebner's division would then follow the armor along a route that would, by now, be cleared of the enemy. At the other end of VII Corps' sector, the 9th Infantry Division, under the command of Maj. Gen. Louis A. Craig, would move into the forest north of the town

3   As per army orders, only one battalion of each regiment was to be committed to the operation.

A US soldier studying the firing mechanism of a captured German MG 42 machine gun, shown here in its tripod "heavy" variant.

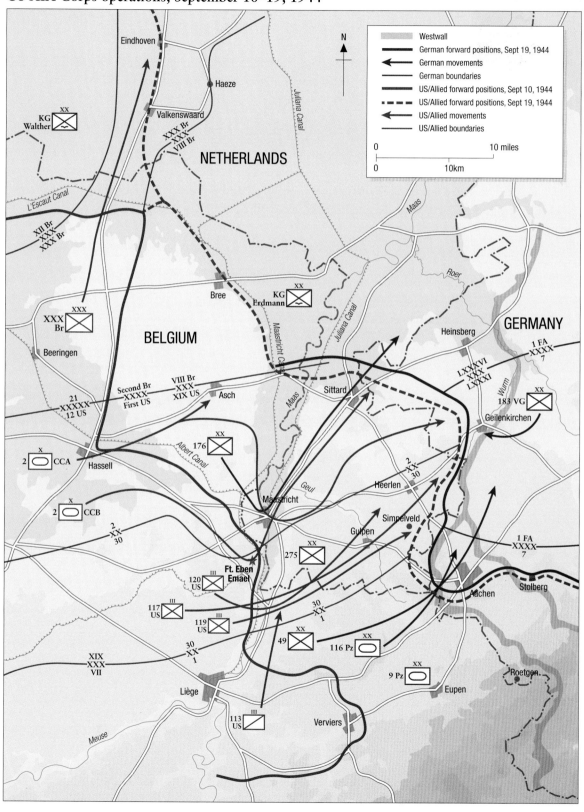

of Monschau, and, while advancing parallel to the armor, would break through the Scharnhorst Line – an outlying section of the Westwall – before continuing northeast, to strike the river Rur (Roer) south of Düren.

To the north, it was left to Maj. Gen. Charles H. Corlett's XIX Corps to fulfill perhaps the hardest mission of all. On one hand, Corlett was to actively support VII Corps' advance, a task that, given the fact that Aachen lay between them, would become progressively more difficult the farther east that Collins advanced, until such time as the city lay in his rear. Corlett's other role was to cover 21st Army Group's right flank as it prepared for and executed its own operations; the difficulty in achieving both of these objectives lay in the fact that Corlett now had only two divisions at his disposal – the 2nd Armored and 30th Infantry – as the 79th Infantry Division had already been transferred back to its parent formation within Patton's Third Army.

Given the progress of the campaign so far, Collins remained convinced that the Germans were firmly "on the run" and that even if the Allies' supply problems were bad then those of the Germans were infinitely worse. All he needed to do in order to secure victory was, to use a 19th-century adage, to keep his sword pressed firmly into the enemy's back. Like Gerow to the south, he firmly believed that this would continue to be a running rather than a static battle and that, if sufficient pressure could continue to be applied to the enemy, VII Corps would be on the cusp of a successful breakthrough, one which would take it safely into the open plain between Aachen and Düren.

As with Montgomery's attempt to secure a bridgehead across the Rhine, Hodges' own operation was based upon faulty intelligence regarding enemy forces. But while the cause of *Market Garden*'s failure would be characterized as the result of an overambitious plan, First Army's mission, however, would founder due to a surfeit of confidence in the ability of its troops to execute their mission, coupled with a complete disregard of the enemy's ability to fulfill theirs. At the highest levels, neither Hodges nor Bradley, nor even Eisenhower himself, could anticipate that First Army was about to commit itself to a battle that would last almost five months, an engagement that would brutally shatter their preconceptions about the ability of the German forces to further prosecute the war.

ENCOUNTERS AT THE BORDER

Before dawn on September 12, Maj. Gen. Maurice Rose, commander of the 3rd US Armored Division – aptly nicknamed "Spearhead" – ordered his Combat Command B (CCB) to move against the enemy forces to his front in order to "determine the strength and dispositions of their defenses," the movement to take place no later than 0800hrs that morning. In turn, Brig. Gen. Truman Boudinot, the CCB commander, directed one of his two combat elements, Task Force 1 (TF1 or TFL after the name of its commander), to probe northeast from the Belgian town of Eupen towards the German border.

Led by the 38-year-old Lt. Col. William "Bert" Lovelady, TF1 was organized around Lovelady's own command, the 2nd Battalion, 33rd Armored Regiment, to which were added the 2nd Battalion, 36th Armored Infantry Regiment (less its F Company); a battery from the 391st Armored Field Artillery Battalion; the Reconnaissance Company, 33rd Armored Regiment (less 3rd Platoon); the 1st Platoon, B Company, 793rd Tank Destroyer Battalion; the 1st Platoon, B Company, 23rd Armored Engineer Battalion; a detachment from the 45th Armored Medical Battalion and a company from the 3rd Ordnance Maintenance Battalion.

At precisely 0636hrs, the attack itself was to be signaled by each of CCB's armored artillery batteries firing a single symbolic round in the direction of the German border but it would still be several hours before Lovelady's men were to leave their encampment due to a series of unexpected mechanical problems. Bedeviled by muddy road conditions and a series of roadblocks and obstructions left behind by the retreating Germans, it was not until 1430hrs that Lovelady's headquarters elements

US infantrymen advance past the wreckage of one of their own tanks.

crested the summit of a winding hill near the Belgian village of Petergensfeld to see a railway track and some station buildings lying some distance before them. West of the station, a solitary farmhouse flew a large Belgian tricolor of red, yellow, and black from an upper story window, while farther to the east stood a small town, many of whose buildings were already sporting hastily improvised white flags as a token of surrender.

For the next quarter of an hour or so, several pairs of binoculars scanned the vista before them in an effort to ascertain the presence and location of enemy troops

German Raketenpanzerbuchse 54 "Panzerschreck." (Ormonde Military History Society)

and, at 1451hrs, with the border of the Third Reich tantalizingly within touching distance, Lovelady finally ordered 1Lt Richard S. Burrows to take his reconnaissance platoon forward and scout the approaches to the town ahead. The remainder of the task force would then follow at a secure distance with Lovelady's mobile artillery being deployed to give supporting fire.

Although the men of TF1 had as yet been unable to identify any hostile troops, they themselves had been under observation for some time by the men of the 4. Zug, Grenadier-Ersatz-und-Ausbildungs-Bataillon 328 (4th Platoon, 328th Grenadier Replacement and Training Battalion), who were occupying positions in and around the railway station and the western edge of the town. Over the last few days, their battalion commander, Oberstleutnant Friedrich Tröster, recently appointed to the command following a medical transfer from the Eastern Front, had hoped to co-opt troops retreating through Roetgen in the face of the American advance to assist in its defense, but in this he had been spectacularly unsuccessful. Nor could he count upon the local Party functionaries who, until recently, had been patriotically vocal about the certainty of the *Endsieg* (Final Victory) but whose duties now took them to places far removed from the fighting such as Düren or – better still – Cologne or Düsseldorf. His only ground for optimism was a promise from his corps commander that a Kampfgruppe from the 9. Panzer Division had been ordered to move up in support and was expected soon.

As such, Tröster had planned to mount his principal defense east of the town, where terrain and fixed defenses would serve to reduce the disparity between his forces and those of the enemy. Given local reports that the German observation platoon was equipped with only limited small arms and a number of light machine guns, and indeed TF1's own after-action reports, it would appear that these men remained in position barely long enough to confirm the size of the American unit before withdrawing through the town to make their report and rejoining their parent company in its battle position.

Cautiously, Burrows' men passed the Belgian farmhouse without drawing enemy fire. and as they reached the railway tracks, they could make out the sign above the station: ROETGEN. They were now in Germany, among the first enemy troops to set foot on German soil since the Napoleonic Wars over a century earlier. Continuing his advance, Burrows sent a runner back to his

TASKFORCE LOVELADY: BREAKTHROUGH AT ROETGEN, SEPTEMBER 12–13, 1944

As part of a general American advance, the 3rd Armored Division's Task Force "Lovelady" was tasked with seizing the border town of Roetgen and from there head eastwards into the Hürtgen Forest.
It was to perform a crucial dual role of both covering the right flank of US forces advancing on the city of Aachen from the west, whilst simultaneously securing a route through the forest itself and into the open plain beyond, a vital staging point for the advance to the Rhine.

ROETGEN

SCHLEEBACH BRIDGE

BK	Bunker
ST	Slit trench
AT	Antitank gun
R	Roadblock
AD	Antitank ditch
CP	Company command post
RO	Radio observation post
AO	Artillery observation post

Note: gridlines are shown at intervals of 1km (1.2 miles).

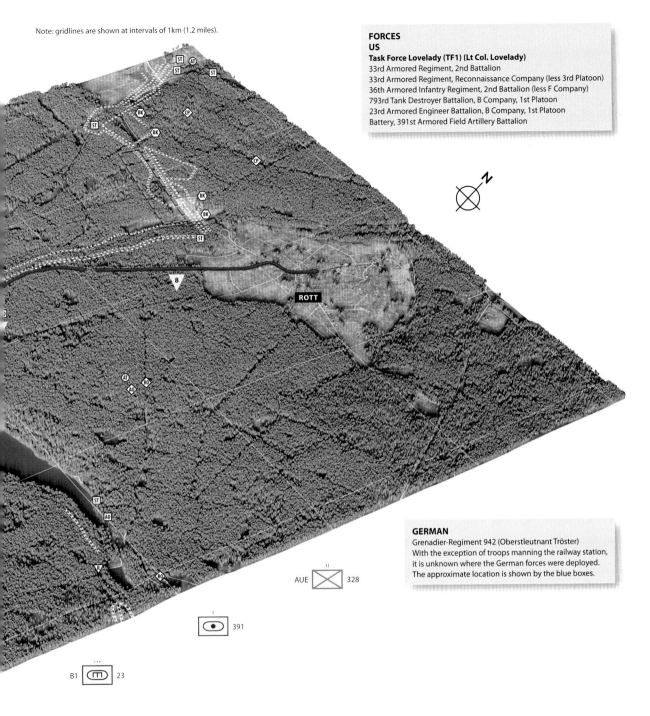

FORCES
US
Task Force Lovelady (TF1) (Lt Col. Lovelady)
33rd Armored Regiment, 2nd Battalion
33rd Armored Regiment, Reconnaissance Company (less 3rd Platoon)
36th Armored Infantry Regiment, 2nd Battalion (less F Company)
793rd Tank Destroyer Battalion, B Company, 1st Platoon
23rd Armored Engineer Battalion, B Company, 1st Platoon
Battery, 391st Armored Field Artillery Battalion

GERMAN
Grenadier-Regiment 942 (Oberstleutnant Tröster)
With the exception of troops manning the railway station,
it is unknown where the German forces were deployed.
The approximate location is shown by the blue boxes.

EVENTS

1. TF1 arrives from Eupen and takes up position above Petergensfeld and occupies a defensive position while a reconnaissance of the terrain ahead is conducted.

2. Reconnaissance Platoon under 1Lt Richard S. Burrows is sent into Roetgen to investigate enemy presence – the German platoon manning the area around the railway station withdraws into town.

3. Having found no sign of the enemy, Burrows continues through Roetgen until he reaches the Schleebach bridge, which has been destroyed by the Germans. As he investigates, he is killed by a German sniper and his troops withdraw into Roetgen.

4. Following Burrows' platoon, the remainder of TF1 enters Roetgen and occupies the town.

5. At night, 23rd AER, B Company, escorted by 36th AIR, D Company, repairs the damage to the Schleebach bridge; Captain Hall of D Company is killed during the firefight.

6. Advancing from Roetgen on September 13, TF1 encounters the first German roadblock – armor and heavy machine guns are brought up to clear the way.

7. Ascending the road towards Rott, TF1 is ambushed by German tanks and AT guns, losing several vehicles before bringing firepower to bear and destroying the ambushing force.

8. TF1 continues on its march to Rott and secures the town.

A jeep of the 33rd Armored Regiment at the railway station in Roetgen.

commanding officer to advise him that no contact had as yet been made and that he would continue his advance into the town.

For his part, once he himself had reached the railway line, Lovelady sent a radio message to CCB headquarters to advise Boudinot of his current location and situation. The latter, in anticipation of such a report, had already ensured that a coterie of news reporters, both civilian and military, was present when Lovelady reported in to confirm his presence in Germany. In this he was not to be disappointed, enthusiastically yelling to his radio operator "Tell Lovelady he's famous! Congratulate him and tell him to keep on going!"

After three years of war and almost 100 days of continuous combat, coupled with the extensive enemy propaganda, the effect of their presence on enemy soil was not lost on the Americans, as William B. Ruth of the 33rd Armored Service Company later wrote, "We entered Germany and Roetgen was the first German city that fell to the Allies, and I am proud to say that the 3rd Armored Division was the first to break the Siegfried Line. Needless to say, we entered Roetgen without the applause that we were used to from entering France or Belgium. Instead, we saw white sheets hung from the windows on all the houses."

Following the reconnaissance party, the remainder of TF1 descended into the valley and moved into Roetgen, the troops spreading out to consolidate their position, thankful that they had escaped the necessity of having to secure the town in bloody house-to-house combat. This was occupation rather than liberation, and with memories of their earlier reception in France and Belgium, none of the American soldiers really knew what to expect. As the tankers moved into the streets, Sgt Robert Laurent noted, "I drove with my armored vehicle in the middle of the main street and it felt like marching in a victory parade through a cemetery."

East of the town, Burrows continued with his mission, but when following the road eastwards towards a local dam – the Dreilägerbachsperre – he found that the bridge across the Schleebach stream had been blown by the enemy.

Dismounting from his vehicle, Burrows moved forward to investigate the damage to the bridge. As he approached the wreckage there was a single sharp report and he fell, victim of an unseen enemy sniper, the first American serviceman to be killed on German soil. The shot that killed Burrows now acted as a signal for a general fusillade and, under a hail of small arms fire, the American patrol withdrew back towards Roetgen.

It was clear to Lovelady that not only could no further progress be made that day, but that also the days of rapid advances were now at an end, for if the enemy were able to barricade and defend every narrow defile, it meant that his troops would need to fight for each and every yard gained, pressing forward in the face of uncertain enemy opposition.

At about 1700hrs, E Company of the 36th Armored Infantry commanded by 22-year-old Captain Almiron P. Hall,

A Sherman tank attempts to pass through a line of *Panzersperren*. This image gives a suitable rendition of the scale of the concrete blocks in comparison to the vehicles they were meant to stop.

Jr, was sent forward in open order, providing covering support for a detachment of engineers whose task was to repair the bridge and render the road suitable for the movement of vehicles. But as the infantrymen reached their objective they too came under an intense fire from enemy positions on the slopes above the road, suffering a number of casualties, one of whom was the unfortunate Hall. Aware that crossing the Schleebach under fire would be a difficult proposition, Lovelady ordered the 36th's D Company to leapfrog their comrades and probe west along the road to Rott to see if progress could be made in that direction. Meanwhile, he ordered up a battery of M7 self-propelled guns to engage the enemy positions under open sights. Under this close-range bombardment it was only a short time before the first improvised white flags were seen amongst the trees, and with

Memorial at Roetgen commemorating the dead, notably 1Lt Richard S. Burrows and Oberfeldwebel Heinrich Brunk. (Ormonde Military History Society)

hands raised in token of surrender, the first grey-clad *Landser* made their way down towards the American positions.

On the road to Rott, the dismounted company soon encountered its first enemy barricade – the road itself being blocked by a tumble of twisted steel girders fixed between two immobilized vehicles. With its left flank buttressed onto the forested hillslope, the roadblock was flanked on the opposite side by a long line of *Panzersperren*, pyramidal structures of poured, reinforced concrete, which would become colloquially known to Allied servicemen as "Dragon's Teeth."

German roadblock constructed from steel girders, forming a continuation of the *Panzersperren*. (Bundesarchiv, Bild 146-1984-051-27/ Lohmeyer/CC BY-SA 3.0 DE, https://creativecommons.org/licenses/by-sa/3.0/de/deed.en, via Wikimedia Commons)

Of differing heights and sizes, these obstacles were placed in deep belts of offset rows in order to create a solid barrier impenetrable to vehicles. The Germans had chosen their position well as the blockage would need to be engaged frontally and – inevitably – under enemy fire.

Lovelady's earlier concerns were soon realized when the head of his column was engaged not only by rifle and machine-gun fire from pillboxes and entrenchments, but also by indirect artillery fire. He was therefore obliged to deploy both tanks and half-tracks to engage the enemy with explosive shells and heavy machine guns. Again, and under this barrage of concentrated fire, it was not long before further forlorn tokens of surrender were seen by the men of TF1. Once again, the engineers were called into

Site of the initial roadblock encountered by Lovelady on the outskirts of Roetgen. (Ormonde Military History Society)

service, this time to dismantle the roadblock, which was demolished by the application of a considerable amount of TNT, the wreckage being towed off the road by tanks.

The American tankers had no sooner surmounted this new obstacle than they were confronted by a fresh challenge. The road ahead was strewn with mines, which – luckily for the GIs – the enemy had had no time to emplace properly, and they were easily cleared with only a minor inconvenience, before the men of D Company remounted their vehicles. Further progress was soon arrested when the head of the column came under heavy enemy fire as the road meandered up a steep hillslope. Forced to advance in single file, four Shermans and a half-track were soon ablaze, but faced by a far superior force, it was inevitable that this could be only a delaying action and German casualties began to mount with the men of Lovelady's command later claiming to have destroyed one PzKpfw V Panther, two 88mm anti-aircraft guns, three antitank guns, and a number of 20mm anti-aircraft guns during the engagement.

As the Shermans continued their advance, a lone Panther emerged from cover intent on enfilading the column, but before it could attack it was spotted by the tank of S/Sgt George Stanko, who, without hesitation, ordered his crew to engage the threat. Stanko's gunner opened fire, and though he failed to destroy the enemy vehicle, it was nonetheless immobilized. Before the panzer commander could react, Stanko quickly ordered six more rounds to be fired into the stricken vehicle, which soon left it a charred and smoking wreck. Observed by both Generals Rose and Boudinot, who had come forward to confer with Lovelady, Stanko's prompt action would later result in his receiving a battlefield commission.

With the road now open, CCB was free to continue with its primary mission of driving a steel wedge through the enemy lines towards Düren, while also fulfilling its secondary mission of supporting the 1st and 9th Infantry Divisions in the execution of theirs. Himself a veteran of the fighting in the Hürtgenwald, historian Captain Charles B. MacDonald's characterization of VII Corps' failure to make significant progress on this first day was as follows, "Not through any great German strength did it fail, but because roadblocks, difficult terrain and occasional resistance held both armor and infantry outside the Westwall until too late in the day for an attempt to penetrate the line."

Captain MacDonald's appraisal could be considered slightly disingenuous in that the same defensive works and arduous terrain over which the fighting took place were facets that the Germans had consciously factored into their defense in an effort to offset the numerical, qualitative, and – above all –

Panzersperren near Roetgen. Note the concrete "lattice" in the background between the trees which has been lowered onto a stream bed to prevent it from being used to outflank the position. (Ormonde Military History Society)

ROETGEN, GERMAN–BELGIAN BORDER, SEPTEMBER 12–13, 1944 (PP. 58–59)

With the fall of Paris in late August, it had seemed that nothing could prevent Allied forces from crossing into German territory unmolested. The Germans were in full retreat and, buoyed by this confidence, many Allies felt the war would be over within weeks rather than months. As part of Hodges' "reconnaissance in force," aggressive patrolling took place across the length of the First Army's front, and on Tuesday, September 12, 1944, the first significant encounter took place when a detachment of Combat Command B of the 3rd Armored Division crossed the German border near Roetgen.

Having taken possession of the town, the men of Task Force Lovelady (TF1) were soon confronted by the realization that the retreat was over and that the Wehrmacht was prepared to mount a defense, having mined roads as established roadblocks to hinder the American advance. After spending the night of September 12/13 consolidating its plan, Lovelady's command left Roetgen early in the morning and ran almost directly into a thick belt of *Panzersperren* (or *Höcker*, 'humps') – more commonly known to the Allies as "Dragon's Teeth." These obstacles of varying

sizes were constructed from layers of poured concrete and offset in order to disrupt or prevent the movement of vehicles, channelling them onto roadways where they could easily be engaged and destroyed.

Here we see men of the 2nd Battalion, 36th Armored Infantry, attempting to make their way through the obstacle, their progress impeded by the German deployment of successive lines of barbed wire (**1**), which has slowed them down enough to present an enticing target for the German troops deployed on the wooded slopes above (**2**). With the troops unable to force their way across the carefully constructed killing ground, the armored infantrymen are forced to take whatever cover they can behind the *Höckerlinie*, giving what return fire they can (**3**), while an M15A1 half-track equipped with quad-mounted .50-cal machine guns has been brought forward to give suppressing fire (**4**) in order to restore momentum in the advance. It was a method that would be used time and time again throughout the campaign when concentrated heavy firepower would be seen as the key to unlocking German defensive positions.

logistical superiority of the attacking forces. Coupled with this, the nature of the battlefield meant that while aerial reconnaissance could yield reliable intelligence when the aircraft were flying over relatively open terrain, the only way to gather information about enemy dispositions in an area of thick forest was "up close and personal," with the opposing troops virtually within touching distance of each other.

The riskiness of Collins' gamble in ordering his most mobile element to advance on such an extremely narrow frontage where each stage of the advance would increase the danger to its exposed flanks cannot be overstated, but it was a gamble that he had been more than willing to take.

The only accurate view from the American side was the gradual understanding that the Germans were clearly trading space for time, hoping to delay the advance in an effort to reorganize their shattered formations and establish a coherent defense. But even this was given little credence as, while they had encountered Walter Model in Normandy when the German armies were in full retreat and survival a priority, they would now be coming up against the Führer's Fireman in the role in which he had shown such brilliance on the Eastern Front, a defensive campaign where he had a totally free hand.

THE IMPERIAL CITY

Formerly the capital of the Holy Roman Empire, by September 1944, the city of Aachen was a skeleton of its former self, its prewar population of roughly 163,000 inhabitants having been almost halved, while the built-up area of the city was now a wasteland of rubble where almost 70 percent of the buildings had been destroyed or rendered uninhabitable by Allied bombing raids. It was a potential battlefield that would need to be fought over inch by inch and yard by yard, a battlefield where conventional maps would be of little or no use as it was uncertain if the terrain features that they described still existed.

Men of the 1st Infantry Division march forward while jeeps tow empty trailers to the rear for a much-needed resupply.

Within the city, governance was maintained on a tripartite basis with a clear delineation of responsibilities exercised by the Kampfkommandant (military commandant) on one side and the civilian and Party authorities on the other. One such decree stated, "The use of roads for the purposes of military operations and those roads being made available for the repatriation of the population must be determined and secured in threatened areas under the direction of the military district command."

This clearly shows that, not only was the military to have absolute priority of movement, but also that the usage of words which could adversely affect morale was to be clearly avoided, with "repatriation" having a more positive connotation than perhaps "evacuation." Indeed, even before American forces were within striking distance of the city, Josef Grohé, Gauleiter (regional Party leader) of the Cologne–Aachen region, had already submitted a formal request to Hitler for permission to begin an orderly evacuation of the civilian population. It would, however, be almost another week before the Führer gave his qualified assent, limiting his approval to "... the areas in front of and in the Westwall ..."

In theory, at least, there now existed a coherent plan for the evacuation of civilians living in those areas which were or would be threatened, but the division of responsibilities and interest had never really been thought through. Instead of complementing each other, they would ultimately engender mutual competition, with each of the entities involved perceiving that their interests had priority and any other concerns should be subordinate to them, even if the written word implicitly stated or suggested otherwise.

One example was the usage of the road and rail network. The authorities needed access to it to evacuate non-combatant civilians, while the Party claimed priority to move its functionaries, generally to areas away from the potential fighting. Finally, the army naturally needed freedom of movement in order to deploy troops as the military situation dictated.

It is unclear if Hitler's vague assent applied merely for the civilians in question to be moved from the potential front line into Aachen itself, or if any displaced persons were in fact to be moved farther eastwards, but in any event the first signs of potential disaster quickly surfaced when a *mélange* of troops withdrawing through the city, troops redeploying for the defense of this sector of the Westwall, and a coterie of "non-essential" Party and governmental personnel all simultaneously tried to loot the city's limited stock of fuel and transport vehicles for their own use. Amidst this chaos, Oberst Helmuth von Osterroht – Aachen's Kampfkommandant – elected to sieve through the ranks of the retreating units and press any without valid movement orders into service for the defense of the city. In this way, the colonel was not only able to cull a force of almost 5,000 men from these scattered units but was also able to equip them by sequestrating weapons from those troops that he had allowed to continue on their way. Irrespective of their usefulness, he urgently needed the reinforcements as he was not only responsible for the defense of Aachen itself and the security of a number of military facilities within the city, but also for a 6–7km (4-mile) stretch of the Westwall.

Initially, the number of troops in Aachen increased slowly but steadily. Firstly, by the addition of those troops whose unauthorized retreat had been recently curtailed, but also by the arrival of the 176. Replacement Division and the formation of a number of independent machine-gun and engineer companies drawn from the remnants of units that themselves had little combat value. All told, the garrison soon numbered something in the region of 8,000 men, in units of varying size and quality, and on the night of September 9/10, these numbers increased still further with the arrival of the newly formed 34. Festung (Fortress) Machine Gun battalion, which was followed the next morning by a locally conscripted defense battalion (*Landesschützen*), and elements of a fortress antitank battalion, the latter unit being able to deploy a number of much-needed 88mm anti-aircraft guns for use against enemy armor. Due to a lack of transport, only 26 of these could be moved to the front line, so the remainder were deployed in and around the Westbahnhof area in order to defend the rail hub against enemy aircraft. Having organized the defense, Osterroht was now relegated from the overall command due to the arrival of the shattered remnants of the 353. Infanterie Division, whose commander – Generalleutnant Paul Mahlmann – now assumed the senior position on the basis of rank. It was a role that Mahlmann was to occupy purely for a matter of hours in that, in anticipation of a major American attack, the reconstitution of the 116. Panzer Division was temporarily suspended and its core elements rushed to the Aachen sector, the remainder being ordered to follow at best speed once the divisional staff had deemed them to be combat ready. As a result of this redeployment, it was therefore the 116th's commander, Generalleutnant Gerhard, Graf von Schwerin, who – due to his possession of a year's seniority in rank over Mahlmann – became the new de facto commander of the local German forces.

Even before he had time to discuss the situation with either of his erstwhile subordinates – especially Osterroht, who had been monitoring the military communications passing via the Aachen telephone exchange for any information that might hint at enemy actions or intentions – any illusions that Schwerin might have held about the position in which he had now found himself were quickly dispelled by incoming reports that enemy troops had already been seen moving through the Aachener Wald, a large forested area to the south of the city, while further, albeit unsubstantiated,

Generalleutnant Gerhard, Graf von Schwerin, Commander 116. Panzer Division.

rumors would suggest that the nearby villages of Eynatten and Raeren were also now both firmly under enemy control. If these reports were accurate, it would place American forces no more than 10km (6 miles) from his field headquarters, and thus within striking distance of a critical section of the Westwall where the defenses were not only thinner than elsewhere, but also covered the principal road to Düren and thence to the Rhine bridges in the Cologne area.

A Kampfgruppe drawn principally from the 60. and 156. Panzergrenadiere was hurriedly put together and quickly thrown into action against the enemy positions in the woods. After heavy fighting, the Americans were forced to retreat and the integrity of the defensive perimeter restored. It was, however, a limited victory as the German infantry lacked both the numbers and firepower to exploit their success and move against the occupied villages. Having gained a respite during which he was able to more accurately appraise the situation, Schwerin, however reluctantly, gave orders that the evacuation of civilians was to cease with immediate effect, using his *Feldgendarmerie* (military police) to clear the road and rail network of refugees and ensure that the non-combatants returned to their homes.

On the face of it, this was naturally seen as an exceptionally harsh measure, as it forced many civilians to remain in a city about to come under attack, but for Schwerin – as the man on the spot – and the officers to whom he reported, there was but one priority over and above the reinforcement and resupply of the German forces and that was their ability to maneuver as the situation required. Heeresgruppe B had suffered horrendous losses in the battles in Normandy and the retreat through Belgium and, while these were to some degree being made good, Model could not afford to commit his limited mobile forces to static engagements. Autumn was approaching and he was counting on a deterioration in the weather curtailing the activities of the Allied air forces, an eventuality which would give him more room to maneuver in every sense of the word.

With the closest American incursion successfully turned back, and the position reinforced by units from within Aachen itself, Schwerin now decided to withdraw his own division and redeploy it north of the city near the town of Würselen from where it could not only cover the northern arc of the defensive perimeter but would also occupy terrain more suited to its effective use while still maintaining the use of the local road network. But before he did so, he drafted a short note that would have profound ramifications not only for the general himself, but also for both combatants and non-combatants in the battles for Aachen and the Hürtgenwald. As the former head of the Anglo-American section of the Fremde Heere West (Foreign Armies West) – a department of the General Staff whose task was to appraise and report upon the armies of those Western powers either in or likely to be in conflict with Germany – Schwerin was fluent in English and he therefore wrote in that language, the text of his note being as follows:

> To the commanding officer of the US Forces occupying the town of Aachen.
> I stopped the stupid evacuation of the civil population and ask you to give her relief.
> I'm the last commanding officer here.
> 13.9.44   (signed) Gerhard, Count von Schwerin
>   Lt.General

It should be noted that the message was written in anticipation of a continued American advance against the city, one that Schwerin simply believed that he had insufficient resources to repulse, and was left in the hands of a member of staff at the central telephone exchange who was detailed to remain behind and assist with the establishment of a civilian administration should the city fall to the enemy. Its intent – as can be clearly seen – was not to surrender Aachen to the Allies nor was it an attempt to declare it to be an open city as had Choltitz in Paris, but instead it was a move to hopefully mitigate the suffering to which his own orders had condemned the remaining population of Aachen and any refugees unlucky enough to have been caught up in the headlong retreat of recent months.

Such was the intent, but what Schwerin could not have known when he wrote it was that a combination of factors – the Allied supply situation, the deteriorating weather, and changes to the Allies' immediate objectives and priorities, not discounting the success of his own counterattack against their penetration into the Aachener Wald – would cause Collins to call off his attack on the city and order Huebner to consolidate his existing gains while waiting for the situation to clarify itself. This naturally meant that there would be no American officer into whose hands the general's note

An American soldier inspects a captured 75mm Pak 40 antitank gun in its concealed firing position.

could be delivered, but when he tried to retrieve it, Schwerin was shocked to discover that the letter was now in the hands of the security services who made certain that its contents were made known to their superiors, with Gauleiter Grohé and other Party officials losing no time in denouncing the general's treasonable actions, using the outcry they themselves raised to paper over the cracks of their own less than creditable behavior.

In Berlin, Generalleutnant von Schwerin was accused of treason against the state and relieved of his military commands, being ordered to immediately hand over his division into the temporary command of Oberst Voigtsberger while his role as Kampfkommandant was assumed by Oberst Maximilian Leyherr, a highly decorated officer who also happened to be the son-in-law of Generaloberst Franz Halder, former chief of the Army General Staff.[4] Schwerin was instructed to report in person to Schack at LXXXI Armeekorps headquarters. Aware that, should he present himself as ordered, he would be shorn of any protection that his current location might afford him and that such foolishness would invariably lead to a noose or a firing squad, Schwerin signaled his intended compliance with the orders but requested permission to first bid farewell to his troops. Permission was granted, but instead of saying goodbye to his men, Schwerin instead informed them of recent events and placed himself under their protection, a request to which they were more than willing to accede.

Despite the fact that Schwerin's unwitting action had now served to threaten the stability of the German position, Model was unwilling to lose the services of an experienced officer at a time of crisis, and instead chose to characterize the whole affair as a regrettable lapse of judgment. Both Brandenberger and Schack immediately joined their commander in composing a testimonial to the count's hereto unblemished service record. In addition, Model tactlessly made a number of pointed observations to

4   Following a change in Hitler's views on the defense of Aachen, Leyherr was removed from the command on October 12 to be replaced by Oberst Gerhard Wilck, commander of the 246. Volksgrenadier Division, which had recently been released to LXXXI Armeekorps.

the effect that not only were Schwerin's actions driven by his concern for non-combatants, who by a combination of military expediency and bad planning had been forced to remain in the city, but also that – in the end – and irrespective of how close the enemy troops might be, the unavoidable truth was that Aachen remained firmly in German hands. He then suggested that there would almost certainly be an inevitably adverse effect on morale should any form of public tribunal be convened which would then reach a guilty verdict. Thirdly, and finally, Model intimated that many of the Party functionaries whose job had been to administer civilian affairs in Aachen had not only singularly failed to observe the terms of the oath that they had taken upon assuming office, but had also damningly chosen to relocate from the city before the enemy had even come within sight.

A tribunal was indeed held, but – and almost certainly as a result of his commanding officers' interventions – its findings were such that Schwerin was deemed to have been suffering from acute nervous exhaustion and, as a result of his exemplary service record, he was accordingly placed in the Führerreserve on grounds of ill-health. In December 1944, and seemingly rehabilitated, he was given command of the 90. Panzergrenadier Division in Italy and then, by year end, had been appointed to the temporary command of the LXXVI Panzerkorps, a position that was to be made permanent on April 1, 1945, when he received a simultaneous promotion to General der Panzertruppen. He ended the war as a British POW.

A CHANGE IN STRATEGY

It was by now clear to Hodges that the whole concept of First Army's advance – predicated as it had been on maneuver rather than combat – needed a complete rethink, and that with the utmost urgency. Up until this point, almost all of the Allies' logistical effort had been directed at keeping the troops supplied with the requisite fuel to maintain the momentum of the pursuit. The problem facing him now was that not only was it was manifestly clear that the German forces had arrested their retreat and were now prepared to stand and fight – if not from a position of strength, then at least from one of near parity – but also that the Allies had stretched their already overburdened logistical tail beyond all acceptable limits and were in the process of pushing it to breaking point. A change in emphasis, increasing the deliveries of arms and ammunition at the expense of the amount of fuel being carried, was indeed possible, if not necessary. But any such change – as Hodges was advised – would still take several days to take effect.

Such delays were inevitable given the necessary changes to First Army's logistical priorities: with every available motor company already pressed into the transportation of fuel not only was there very little "lift" capacity remaining to bring the necessary supplies

This innocuous glass jar and lid are the outer casing of a German Glasmine 43.

US VII Corps operations, September 12–29, 1944

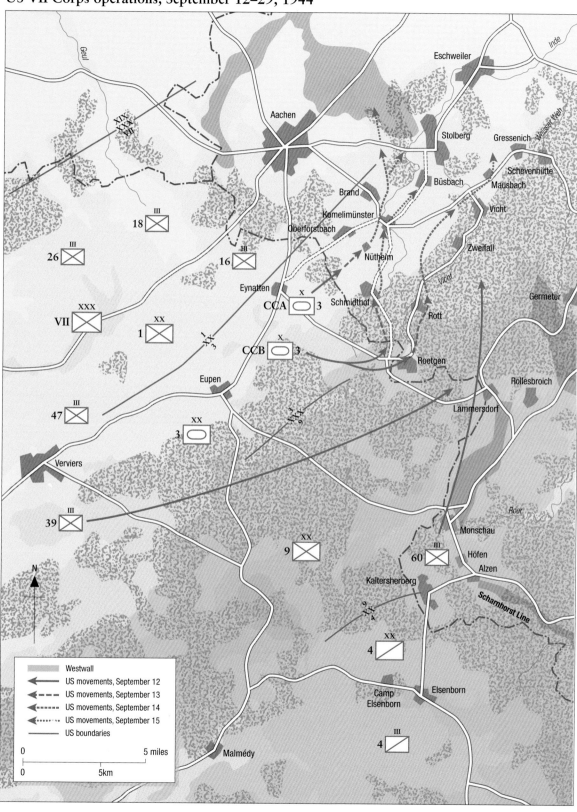

Eschweiler

Inde

Geul

XXX
XIX
VII

Aachen

Stolberg

Gressenich

Weisser Weh

Brand

Büsbach

Schevenhütte

Mausbach

III
18

Kornelimünster

Vicht

III
26

Oberforstbach

Nütheim

Zweifall

III
16

Vicht

Eynatten

X
CCA   3

Schmidthof

Rott

Germeter

XXX
VII

XX
1

XX
1
3

X
CCB   3

Roetgen

Rollesbroich

Eupen

Lammersdorf

III
47

III
9
3

XX
3

III
39

Roer

Verviers

XX
9

Monschau

III
60

Höfen

Alzen

Kaltersherberg

Scharnhorst Line

XX
9
4

XX
4

Camp
Elsenborn

Elsenborn

N

III
4

Malmédy

	Westwall
	US movements, September 12
	US movements, September 13
	US movements, September 14
	US movements, September 15
	US boundaries

0   5 miles

0   5km

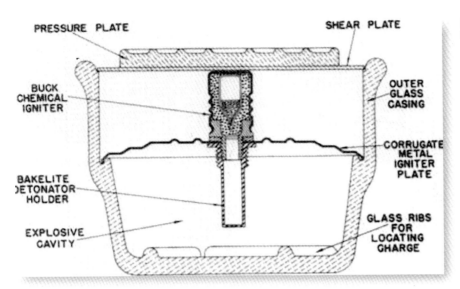

PRESSURE PLATE   SHEAR PLATE

BUCK CHEMICAL IGNITER

OUTER GLASS CASING

CORRUGATE METAL IGNITER PLATE

BAKELITE DETONATOR HOLDER

EXPLOSIVE CAVITY

GLASS RIBS FOR LOCATING CHARGE

Schematic diagram of a German Glasmine 43.

to the front, but also the supply trucks of the "Red Ball Express" – the Allies' principal method of transport at this time – were consuming almost as much fuel during the execution of their mission as they were actually able to deliver to the front line. Although the problem was endemic to all sectors of the Allied Expeditionary Force, First Army was particularly badly hit with Corlett's XIX Corps having already been forced to make a temporary halt on September 9 due to a lack of fuel. Although VII Corps was better off in that particular regard, Collins' troops were still nonetheless consigned to supplementing their rations with those captured from the enemy.

As a result, Hodges had no option other than to implement a short-term system of rationing which, while it could not resolve all of the problems that he faced, would nonetheless be of great assistance until the situation normalized itself. Another consideration was the status of the 5th Armored Division, which had recently been transferred from Third Army, with one wag on the staff commenting that the division had suffered less damage at the hands of the Germans than it had at the hands of Patton himself.

If these problems were not bad enough, Hodges was now confronted by the sobering fact that, in being forced to maintain contact with the formations on either flank, his forces were greatly overextended, indeed – perhaps – dangerously so. Doctrine of the time stated that in an offensive posture, an army corps should occupy a frontage of somewhere between 8 and 16km (5 and 10 miles), depending on tactical deployment and terrain. With three such corps, First Army should have occupied a frontage of somewhere between 24 and 48km (15 and 30 miles) and yet, and as it approached the Westwall, the army was moving on a broad front of almost 130km (80 miles), in places its regiments were stretched perilously thin and gravely exposed should the Germans choose to turn and fight.

Intriguingly, this was what Hodges actually needed. If the Germans stood and gave battle, American fuel consumption would decrease as the troops would have less ground to cover, thereby creating the conditions necessary for increased deliveries of much-needed ammunition. Ideally, once the enemy retreat had ended, they could be pinned and held in position until Allied superiority in every branch of service could be brought to bear and secure an overwhelming victory.

THE HÜRTGENWALD – INSIDE THE GREEN HELL, OCTOBER 1944 (PP.70–71)

With the whole region criss-crossed with narrow winding roads, it was soon apparent to the American commanders that the desired objectives would never be achieved by adhering to the limited road network and that, at some stage, the troops would need to move "off road" and enter the forest. Their preconceptions being dictated by a relatively small green area on their strategic maps, they mistakenly believed that the small wooded area could, and indeed would, be negotiated in a relatively short period of time.

The reality was much different. As the troops began their advance through the closely packed trees, the first thing of import was the realization that their wheeled and tracked supports could no longer act in concert with them and thus their offensive firepower was greatly denuded, which placed them at a significant disadvantage in the form of "encounter battle," in which they would regularly become engaged. Moving forward in what was often an oppressive arboreal twilight, the infantrymen soon discovered their vulnerability to enemy artillery rounds, which, exploding in the upper branches, would augment their killing power by creating a hail of lethal wooden splinters that would fall to the forest floor below.

When under artillery fire, US troops had been trained to present as low a silhouette as possible, which naturally meant having to lie prone. However, in this situation, that put them in the greatest possible target position to be hit by the falling wood or metal splinters. The best procedure was actually to get as close to a tree trunk as possible.

Here we see a combat medic of the 22nd Infantry, 4th Infantry Division, treating a comrade who has been hit by falling splinters (**1**), created by airbursts exploding in the canopy above. Around him, other members of the unit are trying to find cover as best they can – some against the trees (**2**), while others attempt to find shelter behind or under fallen tree trunks (**3**). Others, unfortunately, have been unable to reach cover in time and have succumbed to the danger from above (**4**).

In time, they would see the forest as much of an enemy as the German troops, dubbing the Hürtgenwald as the "Green Hell," or perhaps more emphatically as the "Death Factory."

Rather than engage in a frontal attack on the city, which would undoubtedly result not only in costly street fighting but also the unnecessary expenditure of precious ammunition, Hodges instead elected to render the German position obsolete by ordering XIX Corps to make a demonstration southeastwards from its current position north of the city, while VII Corps would make a reciprocal move from the south, the intention being that the two pincers would ultimately link up somewhere east of Aachen, encircling the city and paving the way for the next stage of the advance to the Rhine. Given that the garrison of Aachen was the largest formed body of enemy troops so far encountered, the remainder of Collins' command was to continue with its existing orders and break through the northern part of the Hürtgenwald and out into the plain beyond.

THE GREEN HELL

Having assembled farther to the west, Maj. Gen. Craig's 9th Infantry Division would now go into action a day later than either of its sister formations, but nonetheless it would be the first American unit to venture into what the veterans of the battle termed the "Green Hell."

Covering an area of almost 90km² (35 square miles), the Hürtgenwald rises from an elevation of approximately 170m to almost 566m (roughly 577ft to 1,857ft above sea level), and is crossed by lines of rolling, often steep hills, punctuated by sharply ridged valleys, watered by several rivers. At the time of the battle, those waters were gathered in a series of dammed lakes that were used for the provision of hydro-electric power, and criss-crossed by meandering, twisting roads that dictated a pattern of linear settlements orientated principally from southeast to northwest. The whole area was covered with farmland around the towns and villages before giving way to an area of thick, dense forest where the trees grow so close to each other,

During a lull in fighting, men of the 9th Infantry Division wait for orders to continue the advance.

Halted by enemy small arms fire, men of the 8th Infantry Regiment (4th Infantry Division) advance behind the cover of tanks.

that their high-reaching crowns compete with each other for the sunlight, creating a canopy that deflected the rays of the sun from falling on the forest floor. For late spring and early summer, the forest is relatively bright, but late in the year, as the days become shorter, the decreasing sunlight has less chance to filter through the close-knit foliage and creates a ground-level area of obscure twilight, where orientation is often difficult and sound distorted.

Ultimately reminiscent of the forests depicted in the 19th-century fairy tales of the Brothers Grimm, it would become a dark and forbidding arboreal world that would soon become as much of a physical enemy for the American troops committed to action within its confines as were the Germans. However, as the first GI's boots trod its paths, this comparison lay in the future, and it would become apparent only when the weather had closed, conditions on the ground had changed, and opposing troops were locked in combat.

Bypassing Monschau to the southeast, and supported by the 746th Tank Battalion, the three regiments of the 9th Infantry Division, entered the Hürtgenwald on the morning of September 14, deployed between Roetgen and Elsenborn. With his command advancing more or less in line abreast, Craig's intent was to use the 39th Infantry – in the center of his line – to initially mask the western approaches to the Schill and Scharnhorst Lines, before pushing ahead to the village of Germeter and opening the road to Düren as it passed through the villages of Hürtgen and Kleinhau. On the opposite flank, the 47th Infantry would perform a similar task, passing along the northern flank of the forest via the village of Zweifall before securing the area around Gressenich and Schevenhütte from where it would not only open up a further approach route to Düren but would also provide valuable infantry support should the 3rd Armored require any assistance in the execution of its own mission. The division's third regiment – the 60th Infantry – was refused, initially to cover the area between Elsenborn and Monschau, before moving up behind its sister regiments, in a position to support either of them as circumstances dictated.

Effectively dividing his regiment into two unequal combat teams, Col. George H. Smythe, commander of the 47th Infantry, elected to take the first of these, comprising his 1st and 2nd Battalions via Rott along the forest edge, where the going was slightly better, while his reinforced 3rd Battalion would protect the main body's flank by advancing deeper into the woods. With the terrain working against friend and foe alike, Smythe's luck held and he was able to reach the village of Mausbach without encountering any of the scattered German forces in the area. He then pushed his 2nd Battalion ahead in order to occupy Krewinkel to screen the continued advance, but the troops were driven back in confusion by a local enemy counterattack. The story, however, was different for his 3rd Battalion, which found its progress constantly hampered by the rough terrain and, at the end of the second day's march – September 15 – the men no doubt held a collective breath when a large body of German infantry simply marched through their bivouac area south of Zweifall, seemingly more intent on reaching their destination than being alert to the possible nearby presence of enemy troops.

Blissfully unaware that a Kampfgruppe of the 9. Panzer Division was also operating in the area, the battalion commander was nonetheless cognizant that his detachment could be detected at any time. Accordingly, he decided to remain in a defensible bivouac for several hours before continuing to Vicht where he established another such encampment under cover of the forest, his intention being to push ahead and occupy Schevenhütte the following day and establish a defensive position there before contacting Smythe for further instructions.

But it was now, even as he planned the attack that would place him in possession of Gressenich, that Smythe's luck ran out, his regiment finding itself at the forward end of a lengthy and vulnerable salient thrust into the middle of the enemy positions. Alerted to the danger posed by this deep penetration of his command area, Generalleutnant Friedrich-August Schack, commander of the German LXXXI Armeekorps, began to marshall his admittedly scant resources in order to dislodge the enemy and restore the integrity of his lines.

With his 1st and 2nd Battalions closed up to the east of Roetgen, and his 3rd Battalion bivouacked at Konzen some 6km (4 miles) north of Monschau, Lt. Col. Van H. Bond's 39th Infantry Regiment had been given what was, on paper at least, the straightforward task of pushing through the Hürtgenwald in order to open up the most direct route through the forest to Düren and, having received their assignments the previous evening, at dawn on September 15, his battalion commanders took what shelter they could from a persistent drizzle as they further relayed these orders to their company officers.

Lt. Col. Oscar H. Thompson, the 1st Battalion CO, had been given the mission of capturing a chain of four villages: Lammersdorf, Vossenack, Hürtgen, and Kleinhau, thereby securing the only decent road through the forest in order that the regiment could consolidate its position before moving on to the main prize, Düren.

US 81mm mortar section sets up for action in the shelter of a captured enemy bunker.

OPERATIONS OF US 39TH INFANTRY REGIMENT, LAMMERSDORF, SEPTEMBER 14–30, 1944

With Roetgen now occupied by follow-up troops, it now fell to the 39th Infantry Regiment, of the 9th Infantry Division, to further exploit the breakthrough and push further into the Hürtgen Forest. Advancing in adverse conditions and with little or no real knowledge of what lay before them, the GIs would receive a bitter foretaste of the fighting that lay ahead, the thick woods of the 'Green Hell' being as much of an enemy as the German troops deployed to bar their progress.

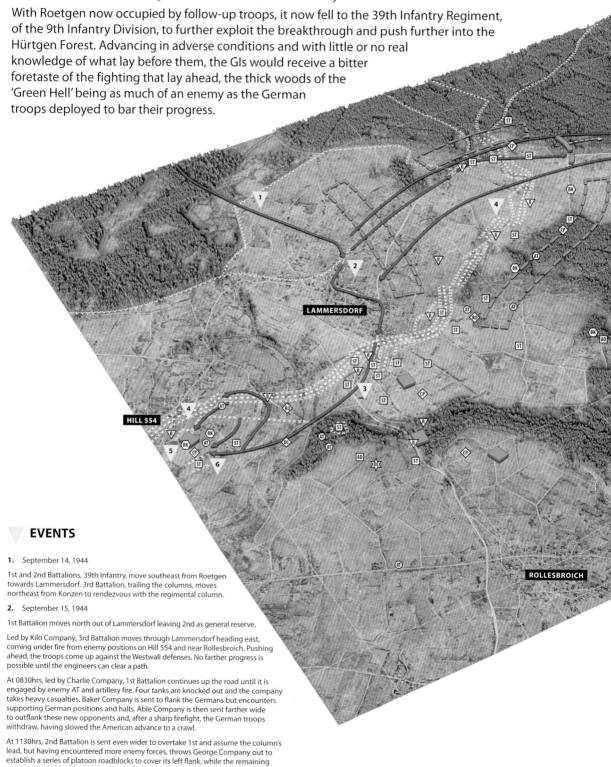

EVENTS

1. September 14, 1944

1st and 2nd Battalions, 39th Infantry, move southeast from Roetgen towards Lammersdorf. 3rd Battalion, trailing the columns, moves northeast from Konzen to rendezvous with the regimental column.

2. September 15, 1944

1st Battalion moves north out of Lammersdorf leaving 2nd as general reserve.

Led by Kilo Company, 3rd Battalion moves through Lammersdorf heading east, coming under fire from enemy positions on Hill 554 and near Rollesbroich. Pushing ahead, the troops come up against the Westwall defenses. No farther progress is possible until the engineers can clear a path.

At 0830hrs, led by Charlie Company, 1st Battalion continues up the road until it is engaged by enemy AT and artillery fire. Four tanks are knocked out and the company takes heavy casualties. Baker Company is sent to flank the Germans but encounters supporting German positions and halts. Able Company is then sent farther wide to outflank these new opponents and, after a sharp firefight, the German troops withdraw, having slowed the American advance to a crawl.

At 1130hrs, 2nd Battalion is sent even wider to overtake 1st and assume the column's lead, but having encountered more enemy forces, throws George Company out to establish a series of platoon roadblocks to cover its left flank, while the remaining companies turn south in order to take the Germans facing 1st Battalion from the rear.

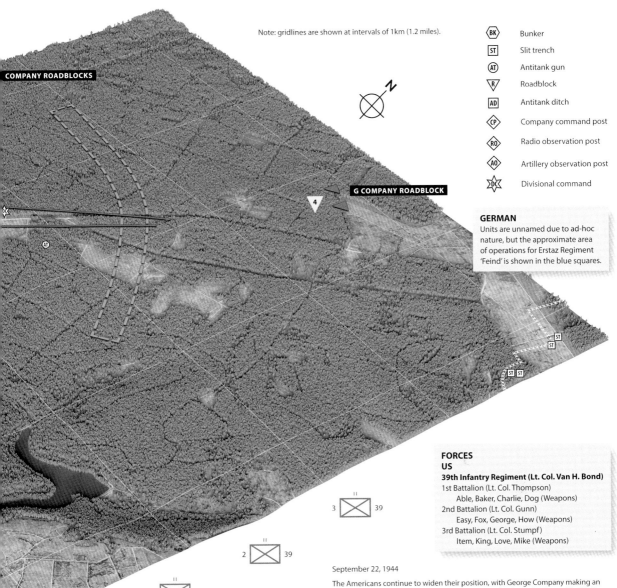

Note: gridlines are shown at intervals of 1km (1.2 miles).

COMPANY ROADBLOCKS

G COMPANY ROADBLOCK

BK	Bunker
ST	Slit trench
AT	Antitank gun
R	Roadblock
AD	Antitank ditch
CP	Company command post
RO	Radio observation post
AO	Artillery observation post
DC	Divisional command

GERMAN
Units are unnamed due to ad-hoc nature, but the approximate area of operations for Erstaz Regiment 'Feind' is shown in the blue squares.

FORCES
US
39th Infantry Regiment (Lt. Col. Van H. Bond)
1st Battalion (Lt. Col. Thompson)
  Able, Baker, Charlie, Dog (Weapons)
2nd Battalion (Lt. Col. Gunn)
  Easy, Fox, George, How (Weapons)
3rd Battalion (Lt. Col. Stumpf)
  Item, King, Love, Mike (Weapons)

3. September 16, 1944

While 1st and 2nd Battalions concentrate on reducing enemy positions and clearing the road north to Germeter, 3rd Battalion continues to feed troops through the fieldworks to its front, in preparation for a further move towards Rollesbroich.

4. September 17, 1944

Able Company is detached to relieve George Company in occupying the roadblocks, with the remainder of 1st Battalion being seconded to the 60th Infantry Regiment to the south.

Having cleared the roadway, 2nd Battalion moves farther south in support of 3rd Battalion, which makes an attack on the German positions on Hill 554. The attack miscarries, although the Americans manage to establish two platoon-sized lodgments, with a view to launching a full battalion attack on the 18th. This new attack is likewise a failure and a combination of casualties and deteriorating weather prevent any further activity.

5. September 20, 1944

Taking advantage of poor visibility conditions, and while regimental artillery and mortars bombarded the German positions, 2nd and 3rd Battalions continue to widen the gap in the Westwall defenses. German counterattacks on Hill 554 recapture lost ground.

September 22, 1944

The Americans continue to widen their position, with George Company making an attack southward to link up with the advancing 60th Infantry Regiment. The 39th's 1st Battalion is subsequently transferred from the 60th to the 47th Infantry.

September 23, 1944

With the weather worsening, American activity is limited to aggressive patrolling and local operations to reduce individual enemy positions. In one instance, Kilo Company had neutralized an enemy pillbox but was able only to force its surrender following the use of improvised satchel charges (of up to 300lb of TNT).

The bad weather continued throughout the following five days when the principal event of note was the reattachment of 1st Battalion to the 60th Infantry. Patrols towards Rollesbroich discovered that off-road movement for armor and heavy vehicles was impracticable.

September 28, 1944

Fox and George Companies combine to make an attack on Hill 554, which – despite heavy enemy fire – was able to secure an advance position for a continuation on the following day, with the anticipation of artillery and aerial support. 1st Battalion reverted to regimental command.

6. September 29, 1944

Beginning at 0935hrs, the American attack began well, but the infantry and armor support became separated from each other and the attack was called off with limited gains.

The following day – and with the Germeter Road secure – 9th Division Headquarters decided that a further advance towards Rollesbroich was no longer required and called off any further advance eastwards, deeming the operation to be a success.

The German Springen Mine S-35. When triggered, the dreaded "Bouncing Betty" would rise to a height of about 1m before exploding and discharging steel balls or similar in all directions.

Led by Charlie Company under a 25-year-old captain, Charles Scheffel, Jr, and supported by a section of four Shermans from the 746th Tank Battalion, the battalion successfully occupied Lammersdorf without incident and was soon on the road to Vossenack, the next link in the chain. The troops had not gone too far when the dull throbbing sound of the Shermans' engines was replaced by the noise of impacting shells as concealed German guns opened fire and in moments had brewed up both the first and last vehicles in the small armored column, trapping the remaining two tanks which tried in vain to get off the road and come into action. Within moments, these too were billowing smoke and flames.

Scheffel's infantry went to ground, trying to take whatever cover they could, but were soon being strafed by enemy mortar and machine-gun fire, unable to move from the roadbed. In an attempt to relieve the pressure on Scheffel, Thompson immediately gave orders for the next unit in the column – Baker Company under Captain Jack Dunlap – to work its way around his left flank, but the relief attempt foundered when it ran into a second German firing position, and with two of his infantry companies pinned, the battalion commander had no other option than to commit his last rifle company, Captain Ralph Edgar's Able Company, to the fighting, being careful to order its commander to swing out farther west before making his turn against the enemy positions.

With a full US battalion fully engaged against an unknown but undoubtedly smaller number of opponents, the Germans continued the firefight until the early evening dusk before withdrawing under the cover of darkness to take up new positions, but the damage had been done. Four Shermans had been lost and Charlie Company badly mauled, with Sheffel himself being one of the numerous wounded. In his later account of the engagement, he recalled:

> Suddenly my world became black and silent. I saw nothing coming. I didn't feel anything. I don't know how long I was unconscious, and then I noticed that I couldn't see anything. I try to move my right arm, but it's impossible. For a moment I think I am dead. Then I wipe my face with my left arm. From my left eye I see blood on my hand. My radio operator is a few inches away from me, his legs are shredded. He is dead. On my other side, by my legs, my despatcher lies lifeless, his head cut off, resting on his chest.

When the fighting had died down, medics started working their way through the dead and wounded, marking those who should receive medical treatment and "tagging" those who had no further need of succor. Badly wounded,

Scheffel would spend time in hospital before a medical discharge saw him return to the United States, his war at an end.

Once the battle site had been secured and casualties evacuated to the rear, Thompson called in the contact and advised Colonel Bond that he would now resume his mission, which was mainly completed without further major incident other than short skirmishes or random harassing bombardment by enemy artillery. But as the battalion began to move around the village of Hürtgen, Thompson received an urgent radio message advising that the 47th Infantry was coming under heavy attack some miles to the west and was requesting urgent assistance.

Despite the arduous nature of the terrain in which his men were operating, Thompson immediately complied with the request and began moving his command towards Mausbach, where his men were instrumental in helping to stabilize the American lines. Given the mounting number of casualties, he was then ordered to take his battalion to the Jägerhaus, a hunting lodge roughly halfway between Germeter and Lammersdorf, where he was to act in tandem with the 2nd Battalion, in effect forming a reinforced battle group, before the whole regiment then withdrew to its starting lines around Lammersdorf.

A similar fate befell the regiment's 3rd Battalion, commanded by Lt. Col. Robert H. Stumpf, as it advanced from Konzen attempting to bypass Lammersdorf to the east. Skirting the edge of the Scharnhorst Line, the fact that Stumpf's three companies – Item, King, and Love – were now having to not only negotiate wire entanglements and minefields but were suffering from the attention of isolated German snipers led him to change his route of march, angling northwest to follow in the wake of Thompson's battalion. Aware of an enemy presence near the village of Rollesbroich, some 5km (3 miles) east of Lammersdorf, Stumpf detached Captain Edward B. Bailey's King Company to reconnoiter the scale of the German defenses in the area, but again the advancing Americans came under heavy fire, this time from a local eminence known as Hill 554 and were forced to withdraw.

US infantry pass through a section of *Panzersperren*.

Col. Charles T. Lanham in conversation with his commanding officer, Maj. Gen. Raymond O. Barton, who is driving his own jeep, aptly named "The Barton Buggy."

Overnight, Stumpf and his company commanders devised a plan of attack whereby the three units would launch converging attacks on the enemy strongpoint in an attempt to split the defensive fire and give them a chance to close and assault the position.

The approach march became disorientated, so much so that tactical coordination was lost and only Love Company was able to put in an admittedly ineffectual attack, which soon foundered. As it commanded the local area, there was no way that Stumpf could afford to either ignore or bypass the German position, and over the next few days, several attempts were made to carry the hilltop, all of which failed. Finally, and after almost two weeks' continuous combat, Bailey's company, now supported by a platoon of tanks, swept over the southeastern slopes and took the hill.

Having previously detached its George Company to establish a number of blocking positions covering the unit's left flank, the remaining two rifle companies of the 2nd Battalion followed in the wake of the 1st Battalion on the road to Vossenack, their mission being to secure a wooded ridgeline northwest of Rollesbroich, the capture of which would not only place them in a valuable position from which to support the regiment's drive on Vossenack and Germeter but, just as importantly, also deny the enemy the use of eminently placed firing platforms from which they could continue to harass the GIs. It was the first experience the men had of fighting in the heavily wooded terrain, and it was only after five days of

"Bunker Busters" – US infantrymen prepare improvised demolition charges for use against enemy fortifications.

hard combat that they were able to secure the western edge of the ridge and that only after George Company been redeployed to participate in the attack.

After a brief respite, Fox and George Companies launched a combined attack to hit the remaining German troops from both sides and were able to clear the central part of the ridgeline so that the entire terrain feature was now in American hands. It was a hollow victory as the depleted companies were able to hold the position for only two days before they were driven off by an enemy counterattack.

Despite having achieved a number of their initial objectives, the men of Craig's 9th Division had – through the course of a literal baptism of fire – learned that the days of headlong pursuit were over and that now they would be fighting in adverse terrain, against an entrenched enemy whose numbers and combat posture could be only estimated. The ordinary GIs were fighting within the scope of a deadly learning process, where the tactical instruction of their basic training had little or no use or application and where improvisation was the key.

US motorized column moving slowly along a muddy, waterlogged road. In the depths of the Hürtgenwald, off-road movement was extremely limited, which enabled the Germans to plan ambushes and roadblocks with great precision.

Training and tactical doctrine had told them that when under enemy fire, in the absence of fixed defenses, the best option was for the individual soldier to represent the lowest possible profile, but in the thick forest with enemy shells exploding within the canopy, airbursts would create long wooden splinters that would fall to earth like spears or javelins from wars of antiquity. Under this deadly hail, the prone infantrymen were soon to discover that they were adopting the worst possible position to avoid death or injury. Experience would soon demonstrate to them that the best cover in these circumstances was in fact to stand as close to the tree trunk as possible as the splinters – it was hoped – would fly horizontally outwards from the explosion before falling to earth.

Again, the troops soon found that they were singularly ill-equipped to assault German pillboxes or bunkers and soon improvised procedures such as the use of concentrated bazooka fire to literally concuss the enemy into submission. The discussion of firing heavy weapons at firing slits or – for the brave of heart – the obstruction of ventilation shafts was doing the rounds of unit scuttlebutt as the troops sought to devise effective methods to deal with the defenses of the Westwall.

With two of his three regiments effectively stalled, if it was to be said that there was a light at the end of Craig's tunnel it was that his third unit – the 60th Infantry – had by now completed its primary mission of clearing the area around Monschau and was now able to move up and support the 39th Infantry in a proposed attack on Germeter, which was due to take place before the end of September. But even this was soon found to be problematic in that, since Normandy, Allied offensive doctrine had been based upon the application of "Mobility, Artillery, and Airpower" and now, with the nature of the terrain in which his command was presently engaged, the current spate of bad weather, and the continuing supply problems, it was unlikely that Craig could rely, with any degree of certainty, on any of them.

The further one ascended the chain of command, the more the problems on the ground seemed to magnify themselves – at corps level, Collins' battle of maneuver had not only ground to a virtual standstill, but in the face of an enemy force of unknown size and capability, and whether or not he was prepared to admit it, he was in danger of suffering a significant reverse unless he was reinforced. One level higher, and with daily reports coming in that *Market Garden* was not developing into the military success that Montgomery had suggested it would be, Hodges was faced with a situation where of the three corps under his command, one had more or less attained its objectives, albeit with significant losses, one – and this was the one in whose success he had placed most faith – had stalled, and the third was split between its conflicting tactical obligations.

By September 28, less than two weeks after First Army's attack had begun, its commander needed reinforcements, fuel, ammunition, and air cover, but above all he needed to modify his battle plan before the enemy could seize the initiative. In order to achieve this, Hodges now decided to "double down" on his previous strategy by redrawing the operational boundaries between V and VII Corps, his intention being to free up Collins' command in order to continue with the push to the Rhine while Brooks (*vice* Gerow) would now assume full responsibility for clearing the Hürtgenwald of enemy troops, while simultaneously covering VII Corps' right flank. North of Aachen, and likewise caught between two stools, Corlett's XIX Corps would continue with its dual mission, with the 30th Infantry Division preparing for its coming role in the encirclement and capture of the city.

At the next command level, Bradley – and thus Eisenhower – was now counting on Hodges achieving the breakthrough needed before the onset of winter, whereby weather conditions would slow down the Allied advance and afford the enemy an even greater breathing space. The Battle for France had been relatively quick and the nature of the German retreat had meant that Allied losses had not been as high as had been anticipated, but unless a crossing could be secured across the Rhine, the coming Battle for Germany could be costly indeed.

STEMMING THE TIDE

Having won the race to the Westwall, the men of Brandenberger's German 7. Armee were now faced with the reality of their situation, that while the enemy had total control of the skies and the first of the promised reinforcement divisions had indeed arrived at the front, theirs would be a reactive defense, making limited counterattacks where possible and where necessary in order to maintain the integrity of their position, keeping the enemy at arm's length The army's three corps were deployed north to south as follows – LXXXI (Schack), LXXIV (Straube), and I SS-Panzer (Keppler). Of these, it was fated that while the initial American attacks would effectively face the US VII and

Soldiers of 1st Infantry Division bring forward ammunition under cover of smoke shells.

XIX Corps against Schack's command, the reverse was true in the south where the US V Corps opposed Straube and Keppler.

On September 18, while VII Corps was attacking to the south of Aachen, German positions north of the city, which were occupied by the 49. and 275. Infanterie Divisions and being attacked by the US XIX Corps, were in danger of being overrun before a timely counterattack by elements of the 10. SS-Panzer Division stabilized the German position.

Three days earlier, Schack received the welcome news that the first of the promised reinforcements, the 12. Infanterie Division (later redesignated 12. Volksgrenadier Division), was en route to his sector. Commanded by Oberst Gerhard Engel, a former adjutant to the Führer, the unit had been refitting in East Prussia when it received orders to entrain for Aachen, where its 40 troop trains would disgorge their cargoes at several railway stations in the vicinity of Jülich and Düren before moving up to the front.

Aware of the positive effect his division could have on the course of the battle, Engel requested permission to commit his troops as a single force, but Schack denied his request on the pragmatic grounds that a single division could deal with only one situation at a time, while its constituent units could deal with several emergencies simultaneously.

With Engel's troops being committed to combat almost as soon as they had detrained, the Germans enjoyed even more local successes when two companies of the Bataillon 2 of Grenadier-Regiment 48 launched a successful attack against troops of the US 47th Infantry Regiment, then occupying Schevenhütte. Attacking at dawn, just as the enemy was rotating the troops in their forward positions, the grenadiers took the village after heavy hand-to-hand fighting, but were later pushed out of the village, abandoning their hard-won gains in the face of an overwhelming American counterattack.

For Schack, it was a day of positives. Firstly, the enemy had been prevented from making further territorial gains, and with the line stabilized, he was also able to withdraw both the 9. Panzer Division and 105. Panzer

SCHEVENHÜTTE, SEPTEMBER 22, 1944 (PP.84–85)

One of the more tangible American successes during the early part of the campaign was when, in mid-September, King Company of the 47th Infantry Regiment (9th Infantry Division) occupied the village of Schevenhütte on the northeastern edge of the Hürtgenwald. Ostensibly, the village's capture meant that the route to Düren and then to the Rhine was now open but, holding the mistaken belief that reported enemy activity in this sector was the precursor to a German counterattack, the US elected not to reinforce this local success. Although it left the outpost isolated from direct support, Smythe's decision was arguably the correct one as Schevenhütte represented not only a breach in the German line but it was also a latent threat to the left flank of the newly arrived 12. Infanterie Division. Aware of their immediate danger, the American soldiers dug in and consolidated their position with improvised minefields. Determined to remove the threat to his command, Oberst Gerhard Engel – the divisional commander – gave orders that the village be taken at all costs, and in the early hours of the morning of September 22, the Grenadier-Regiment 48 launched a battalion-level attack.

From the outset, things went wrong. Firstly, the commander of the lead German company was killed while conducting reconnaissance of enemy positions. His troops then launched a spontaneous attack on the village, disobeying earlier instructions to work around the enemy flanks and instead drove straight at the center of the village with initial, albeit limited, success before they were thrown back with heavy losses – they suffered over 230 casualties compared to less than 50 US, with Engel later commenting that "our troops bled themselves to death." Although Schevenhütte would remain in American hands, the German attack would prove to be an indirect success as it convinced their opponents to consolidate their gains rather than to exploit them, thus gaining more time for additional units to arrive at the front.

Here we see a German grenadier company beginning its ill-fated attack on the village, taking fire from enemy troops firing from positions in upper floor windows (**1**). Although the designation of their parent unit is that of an infantry division, the troops had been re-formed in East Prussia under a new organizational structure and would be retitled as the 12. Volksgrenadier Division in early October. As such, the fighting around Schevenhütte may have been one of the first occasions during the war when Allied troops on the Western Front were to encounter the Sturmgewehr 44 (StG 44) (**2**).

Brigade from the front line for rest and refit, but as a precaution also chose to relocate his own headquarters to Niederzier, 10km (6 miles) to the north of Düren.

Having recovered from the previous reverse, the US XIX Corps renewed its attack on the remnants of the German 49. and 275. Infanterie Divisions, pushing them back in the direction of Geilenkirchen and Jülich before the Germans committed further precious reserves, namely the 183. Volksgrenadier Division and 902. StuG-Brigade which had been hurriedly assembled at Jülich and thrown immediately into battle, both units suffering heavy losses in halting the American attack.

South of Aachen, and desperate to regain momentum, VII Corps now launched a series of attacks in what the Germans mistakenly believed were merely company strength, but which were in fact reinforced combined-arms attacks, tempered by aggressive patrolling on the part of Collins' troops in order to gain crucial information about the battlefield on which they were engaged. For the first time since the beginning of the "reconnaissance in force," the American troops were supported by significant numbers of ground-attack aircraft, generically referred to by the Germans as "Lightnings."

Major-General Charles H. Corlett, Commander XIX Corps.

Despite initial success, Collins' attack soon got bogged down in the adverse terrain, coming to a standstill in the face of several desperate counterattacks by the skeleton German forces, the enforced pause signifying a lull in the combat where both sides stepped back to reconsider their options.

On September 21, following what he referred to as a "conflict with Party agencies," Schack was relieved of command and replaced by General Friedrich Köchling, his fate being undoubtedly connected to the reaction of Party functionaries to his role in the Schwerin affair and the fact that all other officers (Rundstedt, Model, Brandenberger, and even Schwerin himself) were technically untouchable.

REALIZATIONS AND RESOLUTIONS

Although it was clear that the campaign was not developing as had been anticipated by the American planning sessions, First Army and its subordinate corps still rightly believed that the situation before them was a favorable one and would have a positive outcome. The question was, how would this success be achieved?

Prior to crossing the German border, the Allied commanders had been more than aware of the existence of the Westwall defenses, just as they must have been aware that the retreating Germans would stop and fight somewhere west of the Rhine, and if not in a fortified line where the disparity in numbers and equipment would be somewhat mitigated, then where? The fact is that the headlong pursuit across northern France and the Low Countries had possibly blinded them to factors that might have been noted had the pursuit been more measured.

The truth of the matter is that while the army as a whole had averaged some 40km (25 miles) a day since crossing the Seine, VII Corps – for example – had advanced only half that distance during the course of the two weeks since Hodges had issued his initial orders. A change in strategy was required and although the troops would keep pressing forward, this would be more of an act of consolidation while the supply situation improved and the commanding general considered his options.

On September 25, Hodges issued a letter of instruction that made the following provisions:

a.   A change in the boundary between US First Army and British Second Army.
b.   The establishment of a boundary between the First and Ninth Armies, pending the arrival of the latter on the German border.
c.   The partial relief of V Corps' 28th Infantry and 5th Armored Division by lead elements of Ninth Army.

Four days later, he issued a second memorandum which would – in effect – dictate the course of American operations for the month of October and, depending on the outcome, into November. The main points were as follows:

1.   First Army (XIX Corps) would launch limited operations to support 21st Army Group in the area north of Maastricht while the remainder of the army continued in its push to the Rhine.
2.   The boundary with British Second Army was again redefined and would now run on a Hasselt–Weert–Astin–Deurne–Venray–Venlo line, thence along the river Maas to Heinsberg–Erkelenz–Neuss on the eastern bank.

German infantryman firing a Sturmgewehr 44 equipped with Zeiss sights. (Bundesarchiv, Bild 146-1979-118-55/CC BY-SA 3.0 DE https://creativecommons. org/licenses/by-sa/3.0/de/deed. en, via Wikimedia Commons

3.   Ninth Army's VIII Corps would assume V Corps' position in the line, with the current border between V and VII Corps becoming the new boundary between the two armies. Similarly, corps boundaries were moved slightly north, thereby setting new corps objectives: Bonn and Remagen (V), Cologne (VII), and Düsseldorf (XIX).

4.   V Corps was to prioritize the assimilation of VIII Corps into the line, so that it could shift its focus into the Hürtgenwald and clear the forest, while VII Corps' infantry divisions were disengaged prior to the next phase of operations.

5.   VII and XIX Corps would complete the encirclement of Aachen, while the former – with as much air support as could be mustered – would drive through the enemy to their front, the objective being the city of Düren where they would consolidate their position before pushing ahead to Cologne.

On the face of it, the provisions were sensible ones it. As had been seen, First Army had been advancing on too wide a front, which meant that while contact had been kept with the flanking armies it had been nowhere near strong enough to force a breakthrough. With the change in boundaries, and thus immediate objectives, Hodges' chosen instrument – Collins' VII Corps – should have been able to achieve the concentration necessary to guarantee success. The problem, however, was that each of the changes needed to take place in sequence. In other words, in an order that did not compromise the Allied position, which naturally meant that these had to happen from north to south. The issue was therefore that it would take time for VIII Corps to come into the line, and then for V Corps to move north and assume its new position covering the Hürtgenwald, and all of this had to happen before VII Corps could begin to follow its new orders. The Second Battle of Aachen commenced at 1055hrs on October 2, and ended with an Allied victory on October 20.

With American offensive operations temporarily halted, the Germans took advantage of the lull in the fighting to adjust their own deployments. The 116. Panzer had already been taken out of the line, and would now be followed by both the 2. SS- and 9. Panzer Divisions as soon as their current positions could be occupied by fortress units. The "Leibstandarte" and "Hitlerjugend" Divisions were in the process of being pulled back east of the Rhine, while, in a similar move to his opponent, Brandenberger shifted his own corps boundaries, gradually bringing a semblance of order to the German defenses.

From his own headquarters, Model had every reason to be pleased with himself. Firstly, and of most immediate import, the enemy attempt to secure a crossing of the Rhine at Arnhem had been beaten back with significant loss. Next, and more generally, the "combing out" of retreating units had allowed sufficient strength to be deployed against the initial enemy moves. Now, with a steady stream of independent battalions moving up to fill the gaps in the line, there was hard evidence of the Führer's commitment to support him: the arrival of the 12. Infanterie Division in mid-September, followed at the end of the month by the arrival of the newly constituted 246. Volksgrenadier Division,[5] which was deployed directly in the Aachen sector. Gaps had been plugged in the now-stable line, armored formations had been successfully

---

5   The division was engaged directly in the defense of Aachen, with later US interrogation of prisoners suggesting that almost 40 percent of its strength had come from Kriegsmarine or Luftwaffe cadres with minimal infantry training.

withdrawn from combat for reinforcement and refitting, and further reinforcements were still on the way. All that he needed was for the weather to turn and ground the Allied air forces.

For the next two weeks, with VII and XIX Corps besieging Aachen, there was minimal offensive activity in First Army's sector, and with V Corps ordered to move to its new positions, the Allies were now able to see the benefits of an improved logistical chain, whereby supplies were now being partially transported by rail. This gave them a far greater lift capacity, which rose incrementally from 3,500 tons per day on September 23 to 6,500 tons by October 4, a rate which then remained generally constant for the rest of the campaign.

AFTERMATH

The fall of Aachen was to signal even further changes in the American deployments. Arriving from France, the remainder of Simpson's Ninth Army was now slotted into the line north of XIX Corps, which was then transferred to that formation, being replaced on First Army's order of battle by VIII Corps with all army boundaries being amended accordingly.

As the Americans reorganized, so did the Germans, the most notable change being the further withdrawal of armored units – "Das Reich," "Hohenstaufen," and the "Panzer Lehr" – across the Rhine for reformation as the 6. Panzerarmee while, in addition, the 2. Panzer Division was withdrawn to Mönchengladbach.

The flaw in Hodges' revised plan was that it was wholly dependent upon V Corps assuming responsibility for the position in the line currently held by Craig's 9th Infantry Division, a process that was not completed until the end of October, when the 28th Infantry Division filed into position and the 9th Infantry Division (less the 47th Regimental Combat Team) was reassigned to V Corps and withdrawn to Camp Elsenborn, where they were temporarily stood down. A further readjustment of unit boundaries then took place which ensured that V Corps retained the operational control of the 28th rather than it passing to VII Corps when the 9th Infantry came out of the line.

This meant that, for the upcoming operation, First Army's deployment was as follows:

V Corps   4th Infantry Division, 9th Infantry Division (less 47th RCT), 28th Infantry Division, 5th Armored Division.

VII Corps   1st Infantry Division, 47th RCT, 3rd Armored Division.

VIII Corps   2nd Infantry Division, 8th Infantry Division, 83rd Infantry Division, 9th Armored Division.

Given the time needed to effect the above changes, First Army's plan of attack was again delayed, with the push towards Düren also postponed, this time by the exchange of the 9th and 28th Infantry Divisions, which meant that V Corps' movement to

Assortment of German mines retrieved from various locations in the Hürtgenwald. (Ormonde Military History Society)

The front stabilizes, October 1944

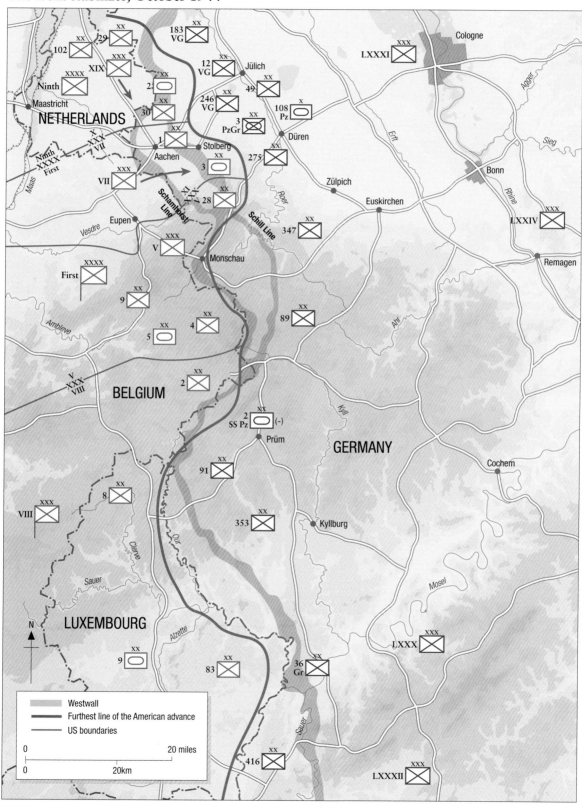

Cologne

LXXXI XXX

183 VG XX

102 XX 29

XX XXX XIX

Ninth XXXX

Maastricht

NETHERLANDS

12 VG XX Jülich

49 XX

2 XX 30

246 VG XX

108 Pz X

3 PzGr XX

Düren

275 XX

Zülpich

Euskirchen

Aachen Stolberg

1 XX

X XXX VII

Ninth XXXX First

VII XXX

3 XX

28 XX XX XXX

Schill Line

347 XX

LXXIV XXX

Schamhorst Line

Eupen

Vesdre

V XXX

Monschau

Bonn

Rhine

Remagen

First XXXX

9 XX

Ambleve

5 XX

4 XX

89 XX

Ahr

Erft

Agger

Sieg

V XXX VIII

BELGIUM

2 XX

2 SS Pz XX (-)

Prüm

GERMANY

Kyll

Cochem

91 XX

8 XX

VIII XXX

353 XX

Kyllburg

Clerve

Our

Sauer

Mosel

N

LUXEMBOURG

Alzette

9 XX

83 XX

36 Gr XX

LXXX XXX

Sauer

416 XX

LXXXII XXX

	Westwall
	Furthest line of the American advance
	US boundaries

0 ——————— 20 miles

0 ——————— 20km

seize the area around Germeter–Vossenack–Schmidt would begin only on November 1, almost a week after it had been ordered.

To date, the campaign had been a learning experience for the American troops, and is best summarized by an extract from First Army's own war diary:

> The month of October had seen the remarkable comeback by Heeresgruppe B. Only a matter of weeks before, a defeated and disorganized force had retreated several hundred miles across France and Belgium to the borders of the Reich. Yet, in that short space of time, it had reorganized sufficiently enough so as to prevent a major breakthrough through the West Wall to the Rhine. This remarkable military feat could be attributed to two things: The existence of a considerable number of fortress battalions, the existence of which the enemy had cleverly concealed, and a flexible system with divisional organization and replacements.

What would come, when V Corps launched its probing attack on November 1, could only be anticipated in so far as it was clear to the Allies that the route through the Hürtgenwald was now barred by a determined and entrenched enemy, and that in order to progress to the Rhine, they would need to fight every inch of the way. What they could not know beforehand was the exact nature of that fighting, the length of time it would take for them to attain their objectives, and the scale of the losses that they would incur in doing so. However, it would not be long before they would find these out through bitter experience.

Maj. Gen. James M. Gavin, commander of the US 82nd Airborne Division, which had just participated in Operation *Market Garden* and whose men would eventually be committed to the fighting in the Hürtgen, would later unequivocally state in his memoirs that – in his considered opinion – the Hürtgenwald was an unnecessary battle that would at best have never been fought.

The tip of the spearhead – vehicles of the 3rd Armored Division caught in a traffic jam on one of the limited roads traversing the battlefield.

FURTHER READING

Ambrose, Stephen E., *Citizen Soldiers: The US Army from the Normandy Beaches to the Bulge to the Surrender of Germany (June 7 1944 – May 7 1945)*, Simon & Schuster: New York (1997)

Citino, Robert M., *The Wehrmacht's Last Stand: The German Campaigns of 1944–5*, University Press of Kansas: Lawrence, KS (2017)

Currey, Cecil B., *Follow Me and Die: The Destruction of an American Division in WW2*, Stein and Day: New York, NY (1984)

Eisenhower, Dwight, *Crusade in Europe*, William Heinemann: London (1948)

Görlitz, Walter, *Model: Strategie der Defensive*, Bastei Lübbe Verlag: Bergisch Gladbach (1977)

Greenwood, John T., *Normandy to Victory: The War Diary of General Courtney H. Hodges (ed.) and the First US Army*, University Press of Kentucky: Lexington, KY (2008)

Hastings, Max, *Armageddon: The Battle for Germany, 1944–45*, Pan Macmillan: London (2004)

Higgins, David R., *The Roer River Battles: Germany's Stand at the Westwall 1944–45*, Casemate Publishers: Havertown, PA (2010)

Kaeres, Kurt, *Das verstummte Hurra: Hürtgenwald 1944–45* (2nd Ed), Helios Verlag: Aachen (2002)

Keilig, Wolf, *Rangliste des Deutschen Heeres 1944/45*, Verlag Hans-Henning Podzun: Bad Hauheim (1955)

Kuffner, Alexander, *Zeitreiseführer Eifel 1933–45*, Helios Verlag: Aachen (2007)

MacDonald, Charles B., *The Battle of the Huertgen Forest*, J.B. Lippincott & Co: Philadelphia & New York (1963)

MacDonald, Charles B., *The Siegfried Line Campaign*, Whitman Publishing: Atlanta, GA (2012)

Margaritis, Peter, *Countdown to D-Day: The German High Command in Occupied France, 1944*, Casemate Publishers: Oxford (2019)

Miller, Edward G. A., *Dark and Bloody Ground: The Hürtgen Forest and the Roer River Dams 1944–45*, Texas A&M University Press: College Station, TX (1995)

Monnartz, Rainer, *Hürtgenwald 1944–5: Historischer Tourenplaner* (2nd Ed), Helios Verlag: Aachen (2022)

Nash, Douglas E., *Victory Was Beyond Their Grasp: With the 272nd Volksgrenadier Division from the Hürtgenwald to the Heart of the Reich*, Casemate Publishers: Oxford (2015)

Öse, Dieter, *Entscheidung im Westen: Der Oberbefehlshaber West und die Abwehr der alliierten Invasion*, Deutsche Verlags-Instalt: Stuttgart (1982)

Pereira, Joseph M. & Wilson, John, *All Souls Day: The World War II Battle and the search for a lost US Battalion*, Potomac Books: Nebraska (2020)

Pröhuber, Karl-Heinz, *Volksgrenadier Divisionen, Eine Studie – Band 1*, Helios Verlag: Aachen (2018)

Schramm, Percy, *Kriegstagebuch des OKW: Eine Dokumentation (ed.) Band 7/8 – 1944–45*, Weltbild GmbH: Augsburg (2005)

Threuter, Christina, *Westwall: Bild und Mythos*, Michael Imhof Verlag: Petersberg (2009)

Többicke, Peter, *Militärgeschichtlicher Reiseführer Hürtgenwald* (2nd Ed), E. S. Mittler & Sohn: Hamburg (2001)

Trostorf, Albert, *Lest We Forget (Part 6) – The 1st Infantry Division in the Battles for Aachen – Hürtgen Forest 1944 – Roer to Rhine Campaign 1945*, privately published

Weigley, Russell F., *Eisenhower's Lieutenants: The Campaigns of France and Germany 1944/45* (2 vols), Indiana University Press: Bloomington, IN (1981)

Whiting, Charles, *Bloody Aachen*, Military Heritage Press: New York, NY (1976)

Whiting, Charles, *The Battle of the Hürtgen Forest*, Spellmount Ltd: Staplehurst (2000)

Yeide, Harry, *The Longest Battle: September 1944 to February 1945 From Aachen to the Roer and Across*, Zenith Press: St. Paul, MN (2005)

Zumbro, Derek S., *Battle for the Ruhr: The German Army's Final Defeat in the West*, University Press of Kansas: Lawrence, KS (2006)

INDEX

Figures in **bold** refer to illustrations.